ParentWise

ParentWise

LEN McMILLAN

REVIEW AND HERALD® PUBLISHING ASSOCIATION
HAGERSTOWN, MD 21740

The author assumes full responsibility for the accuracy of all facts and quotations as cited in this book.

Texts credited to NIV are from the *Holy Bible, New International Version*. Copyright © 1973, 1978, 1984, International Bible Society. Used by permission of Zondervan Bible Publishers.

Bible texts credited to RSV are from the Revised Standard Version of the Bible, copyright © 1946, 1952, 1971, by the Division of Christian Education of the National Council of the Churches of Christ in the U.S.A. Used by permission.

Verses marked TLB are taken from *The Living Bible*, copyright © 1971 by Tyndale House Publishers, Wheaton, Ill. Used by permission.

This book was
Edited by Richard W. Coffen
Designed by Bill Kirstein
Cover art by Helcio Deslandes
Cover photo by Todd Park
Typeset: 11.2/13.2 Sabon

PRINTED IN U.S.A.

98 97 96 95 94 93   10 9 8 7 6 5 4 3 2 1

Library of Congress Cataloging in Publication Data
McMillan, Len D., 1938-
    Parentwise / Len McMillan.
        p.   cm.
    1. Family—religious life.   2. Parenting—religious aspects—
Christianity.   3. Seventh-day Adventists—Membership.
4. Adventists—Membership.   5. Sabbatarians—Membership.   I. Title.
BX6154.M39   1993
248.8'45—dc20   92-33309
                                                      CIP

ISBN 0-8280-0687-3

Contents

CHAPTER 1

Ozzie and Harriet Have Left Town!
(The New American Family)

> *"Who are my mother and my brothers?"* he asked. Then he looked at those seated in a circle around him and said, *"Here are my mother and my brothers! Whoever does God's will is my brother and sister and mother"* (Mark 3:33-35, NIV).

As a teenager in the 1950s I grew up watching Ozzie and Harriet Nelson on our black-and-white television. Their younger son, Ricky, was one of my idols. Each week millions of American households tuned in to watch the Nelson family, which they accepted as *the* model of family life. Ozzie went off to work, and Harriet stayed home to care for the house and kids. Older brother picked on younger brother (but was always there for him), and all seemed safe and sane in the Nelson household.

Somewhere in America's past was this wonderful, nearly perfect small town filled with wonderful, nearly perfect families. Frank Capra depicted it on film. Norman Rockwell captured it on canvas. Singers reminisced about it in *Oklahoma!* and in Bruce Springsteen's songs. American TV viewers saw it on *Make Room for Daddy, Father Knows Best, The Donna Reed Show, Leave It to Beaver,* and, of course, *Ozzie and Harriet.* It was an ideal community in which all the people knew their neighbors and in which families had roots that were more than three generations deep in that same community.

If you don't remember Ozzie and Harriet, don't despair. It just means you probably moved to town after the Nelsons departed. Perhaps you remember *The Waltons* or the people in *Happy Days.* Maybe you moved to town more recently. If so, you may have moved next door to *The Golden*

Girls or an *Empty Nest*. If your orientation is *thirtysomething*, your role model is more likely Bill Cosby than Ozzie Nelson. Now Mom and Dad both nurture separate careers while raising a family at the same time.

Which of these models, do you think, represents the Christian family?

Actually the idea of Father bringing home the paycheck and Mother raising the family is a rather recent innovation. It certainly is not a biblical concept. In fact, Proverbs 31 extols the working woman as the perfect wife and mother. She is gainfully employed in real estate, farming, textiles, and merchandising along with all her other duties as wife and mother. This woman is truly an outstanding entrepreneur.

The Bible makes many references to family life, but seldom are the families modeled after Ozzie and Harriet. It speaks of large extended families numbering in the hundreds (Abraham's). It speaks of a daughter-in-law/mother-in-law relationship that continues to function as family after the death of both spouses (Ruth's and Naomi's). It views a brother and two sisters as family (Mary, Martha, and Lazarus). A budding young preacher's family consisted of his mother and grandmother because his father was not of the same faith (Timothy). Even Jesus Himself was familiar with a single-parent family, since one can infer from the evidence that Joseph died before Jesus reached His early teens.

Actually the idea of Father bringing home the paycheck and Mother raising the family is a rather recent innovation. It certainly is not a biblical concept.

During the Middle Ages and into the eighteenth century the family served as an economic unit in which the entire household worked to provide food and shelter. It also served as a vehicle for the transmission of property from generation to generation. The medieval family was hardly a shelter or refuge at the end of a long day. More accurately, the family was an economic force and legal entity necessary for survival.

With the Industrial Revolution the face of Western culture changed dramatically. Seemingly overnight we switched from an agricultural society to one of machines and factories. Yet this revolution added only cosmetic changes to the family for 100 years. The family that used to work together from dawn to dusk in the fields now worked together from dawn to dusk in the factories. It was difficult to earn a living. Somehow we have come to view those as the "good old days," and some may even shed a nostalgic tear over their demise. An unknown poet offers a more accurate snapshot of the past:

Grandmother, on a winter's day,
Milked the cows, and fed them hay,
Slopped the hogs, saddled the mule,
And got the children off to school.
Did a washing, mopped the floors,
Washed the windows, and did some chores.
Cooked a dish of home-dried fruit,
Pressed her husband's Sabbath suit,
Swept the parlor, made the bed,
Baked a dozen loaves of bread,
Split some firewood, and lugged in
Enough to fill the kitchen bin.
Cleaned the lamps, and put in oil,
Stewed some apples she thought might spoil.
Churned the butter, baked a cake,
Then exclaimed, "For goodness sake,
The calves have got out of the pen."
Went out and chased them in again.
Gathered the eggs, and locked the stable,
Back to the house and set the table,
Cooked a supper that was delicious,
And after washed up all the dishes.
Fed the cat and sprinkled the clothes,
Mended a basketful of hose,
Then opened the organ and began to play
"When You Come to the End of a Perfect Day."

It took a world at war (for a second time in the same century) to dramatically alter the conception of the American family. After World War II the middle-class family unit was given a luxury previously reserved for only the rich. For the first time in history middle-class America could live comfortably on one salary. During this time of relative prosperity Ozzie and Harriet Nelson moved into small-town USA and made an indelible imprint on an entire generation. Some still mourn their departure.

Ironically, many Christians somehow came to believe—or maybe assume—that Ozzie and Harriet were Bible characters, that the Nelsons somehow represented the "traditional" family. Actually, what we call the "traditional" family is barely two generations old. "Family" is difficult to define, since it has so many definitions. Webster offers more than 20. The U.S. Census Bureau defines family as "two or more persons related by birth, marriage, or adoption who reside in the same household."

In Scripture a family exists by birth, marriage, adoption, or choice. In fact, family exists whenever a particular group thinks or feels like it is family. Such is the family of God. Why, then, do we refer to mother, father, and two kids as "traditional"?

After World War II the middle-class family unit was given a luxury previously reserved for only the rich. For the first time in history middle-class America could live comfortably on one salary. During this time of relative prosperity Ozzie and Harriet Nelson moved into small-town USA and made an indelible imprint on an entire generation. Some still mourn their departure.

Family includes communities with a common bond: brothers and sisters in Christ, singles, couples, parents, children, senior citizens, teens, newlyweds, widowed, divorced, natural children, adopted children, stepchildren, aunts, uncles, grandparents, cousins, in-laws. Family is defined by its members, not by society or a dictionary.

God created the first family in the Garden of Eden. Initially it was composed of a single individual and his Creator. God then made a "helper fit for him," and the circle of relationships increased. Family in Eden can be defined by words such as "mutuality" (both shared the garden and its upkeep), "interdependence" (they looked out for each other . . . usually), "equality" (one did not lord it over the other), and "parenting" ("Be fruitful and multiply").

We have come a long way since the Garden of Eden. Unfortunately, it has been in the wrong direction. Today's families find it difficult to live up to the example of Ozzie and Harriet, much less that of Adam and Eve in the garden. Sin brought sweat to the brows of the first family, and today economic pressures put modern families under stress. We thought Social Security would relieve some of the economic stress by caring for the elderly members of our families. But today it is our young families who are under the most financial pressure and are suffering through lingering poverty. Parenting today forces most mothers into the workplace. The number of two-income families has doubled in the past 20 years. In fact, three out of four families in which the husband is under age 45 have two wage earners. This often brings tremendous stress as the parents seek to balance priorities between jobs, spouse, and children.

One father recalls the time when his son's nursery school teacher asked him to visit the class. After finishing his discussion with

We have come a long way since the Garden of Eden. Unfortunately, it has been in the wrong direction.

the teacher, he lingered to observe a group of boys, including his own son, who sat in a circle nearby. Their conversation went something like this:

Child A: "My daddy's a doctor, and he makes a lot of money, and we have a swimming pool."

Child B: "My daddy's a lawyer, and he flies to Washington and talks to the president."

Child C: "My daddy owns a company, and we have our own airplane, and we can fly anywhere we want."

Then his own son, with a great deal of pride, blurted out, "My daddy is here!" and gave his father a big smile and a little wave. The visible sign of a parent present at an important event in a child's life is worth more than all the bravado that children use to fill the empty chair reserved for that parent.

Today's families are also on the move. The average family moves every five years, which prevents it from sinking roots in the community. Today's family is like a tumbleweed. Just about the time it matures it loses its roots.

One young family in transition found themselves living in cramped hotel quarters near a military base where the father was stationed. Because of a housing shortage there did not appear to be an immediate solution to their dilemma. One day a friend said to the 6-year-old daughter, "Isn't it too bad that you don't have a home?"

The daughter quickly responded, "Oh, we have a home. We just don't have a house to put it in!"

The extended family spoken of in Scripture is almost unheard-of in today's Western world. Besides being on the move, individuals today are making less and less commitment to anything, whether it be to family, community, church, or employer. One divorced baby boomer summed it up well: "I think my picture of family when I was growing up was very much like my mom and dad's. Being together with three kids, both working, and having a church community and a social circle of friends.

Today's family is like a tumbleweed. Just about the time it matures it loses its roots.

"Right now, I'm feeling fairly isolated from family and friends with whom I've had a lot of history. I realize a big part of that was leaving the church and a marriage, with the friends that go with them."

Role ambiguity also creates problems for today's families. In years past a woman's work was clearly distinct from a man's work. This is no longer true, and children are sometimes confused by their role models.

A little boy and girl were trying to decide what game to play. The little boy suggested, "I have an idea! Let's play baseball."

But the little girl said, "Oh no, I wouldn't want to do that; baseball is a boy's game. It's not feminine to run around on a dusty vacant lot. No, I wouldn't want to play baseball."

Thinking for a moment, the little boy replied, "OK, then, let's play football."

"Oh, no, I wouldn't play football," the little girl responded. "That's even less feminine. I might fall and get dirty. No, that's definitely not a girl's game."

"Well, OK," the little boy mused, "I'll tell you what—I'll race you to the corner and back!"

"No, no!" exclaimed the little girl. "Girls don't run and get all sweaty and stuff. Girls play quiet games. Girls should never race with boys."

The boy scratched his head, trying to think of what they might do. Finally he tentatively suggested, "Then let's play house."

"Great!" exclaimed the little girl. "I'll be the daddy!"

What are the proper roles of male and female? Who determines the duties of mommy and daddy? Who takes time off work when the children are sick? Who pursues the primary career in the family? What happens when both parents actively pursue a primary career? Who becomes the primary parent? What is happening to the family in America?

Cross-cultural studies show that U.S. parents spend less time with their children than parents in almost any other country. Although in the recent past both Russian parents worked and Russian children spent a great deal of time in family collectives, emotional ties between children and parents were stronger and the time spent together was considerably greater than in America. There is relatively little juvenile delinquency in Russia. Some Russian fathers have said they would never let a day go by without spending two hours with their sons.

Cross-cultural studies show that U.S. parents spend less time with their children than parents in almost any other country.

If parents are not spending time with their children, who will be their role models for human sexuality and responsible sexual behavior? The media bring so much illicit sex into the home that some children are beginning to view it as the norm. Many families depend upon TV to be an electronic baby-sitter, but who teaches the children that afternoon soaps do not exemplify proper role modeling? Who tells them that "sleeping around" is not the norm for an adult? For some, home is more like a zoo than a family.

A few years ago the family was formed in this manner:

> First comes love.
> Next comes marriage.
> Then comes Mary with a baby carriage!

But the sequel for today's family reads like this:

> First comes love.

Next comes Mary with a baby carriage!
Then Mary moves in with John.
Eventually comes marriage.
Then John and Mary get a divorce.

"To gain a proper understanding of the marriage relation is the work of a lifetime. Those who marry enter a school from which they are never in this life to be graduated. However carefully and wisely marriage may have been entered into, few couples are completely united when the marriage ceremony is performed. The real union of the two in wedlock is the work of the afteryears."

John moves in with Sandra and her two boys.
Mary takes the baby.
Then Mary meets Ralph,
Who is divorced but has three children.
Mary and Ralph get married.
Now Mary's baby has a mother,
    father,
    stepmother,
    stepfather,
    five brothers and sisters,
    four sets of grandparents,
    and countless aunts and uncles.

Soon Mary is pregnant again!

During the past 10 years one of every two marriages has ended in divorce. Most of the people involved have remarried. Six out of 10 who have remarried have divorced again. And the list goes on and on . . . and on!

Pollster Louis Harris made headlines when he announced that these statistics were misleading and that the media were using them out of context. Harris went on to explain that those statistics did not include *all* marriages, but only those marriages of the past decade. When all marriages are considered, only one in eight actually ends in divorce.

I guess that is supposed to be good news, but I find it extremely difficult to rejoice over those statistics. The family as exemplified by Ozzie and Harriet is in deep trouble. The Nelsons represent a mere 6 percent of our total population today. What can we do?

Almost 100 years ago a Christian writer offered some inspired counsel that I believe could reverse these statistics if we would only implement her philosophy:

"To gain a proper understanding of the marriage relation is the work of a lifetime. Those who marry enter a school from which they are never in this life to be graduated. However carefully and wisely marriage may have been entered into, few couples are completely united when the marriage ceremony is performed. The real union of the two in wedlock is the work of the afteryears" (Ellen G. White, *The Adventist Home*, p. 105).

Some studies indicate that 70 percent of all men and 50 percent of all women have extramarital affairs. The divorce rate among Christians approximates that of the general populace. Somehow, we have failed to model family and marriage to an entire generation. Yet pollster Harris reports that 94 percent [of 3,001 persons polled] are highly satisfied with their family relationships. Furthermore, Harris reports, 86 percent said they are happy with the support they receive from family members during a crisis, and only 20 percent are unhappy with their family life.

With teen pregnancies, drug use, and delinquency at all-time highs, evidently some parents polled failed to inform their teenage children about the happy home in which they were living.

Ten years ago the National Research Bureau, Inc., reported that 28 percent of runaway children in America were actually forced out of their homes by their parents. Of the more than 22,000 Americans listed as missing, an astounding 79 percent were under the age of 18. Divorce was a major factor in the rising number of abandoned teens. Evidently many parents were more concerned with caring for their own needs than the needs of their children. The report ended with these words: "We have been so anxious to give our children what we didn't have that we have neglected to give them what we did have" (*Encounter*, May 1982).

Have we successfully lowered the divorce rate during the past 10 years? Are there fewer single-parent families today? The answer is an emphatic no! Likewise, the number of juveniles on the street continues to rise, as well as a significant increase in child abuse. One in six children is physically abused, and one in seven is sexually abused" (James Patterson and Peter Kim, *The Day America Told the Truth*, p. 125).

Such statistics should be viewed as a national disgrace!

Chemical dependency brings added stress to today's families. Few families are entirely free from this devastating problem. Children have grown up as codependents, and now are fathers and mothers who transmit these same dysfunctional tendencies to their children. Christian families are especially vulnerable to such dysfunctional characteristics, since they often attempt to hide the problem from both church and community.

Standards and values are changing. The generation gap has turned into a generation chasm. What was once considered pornography by our parents is now general fare in family magazines and sports journals. Answers to moral questions have become blurred. We live in an age of pomp over pithiness, charisma over content, style over substance. This has become a time when who we are seems less important than who people think we are.

Yet this behavior is really not unique to our generation. In biblical times the Pharisees championed charisma over content. They exuded purity and holiness when, in fact, they were merely the forerunners of "dress for success." Jesus was not misled by their tailored garments and outward piety. He referred to them as "whitewashed tombs."

We live in an age of pomp over pithiness, charisma over content, style over substance. This has become a time when who we are seems less important than who people think we are.

Even the language we use today is carefully conditioned so as to give no connotation of good or evil. Euphemistic phrases can seemingly turn wrongs into rights. What used to be "living in sin" has now become a "meaningful relationship." What used to be "chastity" has now become "neurotic inhibitions." What used to be "self-indulgence" has now become "self-fulfillment." What used to be black-and-white has now become desirable shades of designer gray.

"There is absolutely no moral consensus in the 1990s" (*ibid.*, p. 25).

What hope is there for Christian families as we enter our second millennium? Scripture makes it quite clear that one of the primary functions of family is the transmission of values from one generation to the next.

"And these words which I command you this day shall be upon your heart; and you shall teach them diligently to your children, and shall talk of them when you sit in your house, and when you walk by the way, and when you lie down, and when you rise" (Deut. 6:6, 7, RSV).

Some would say that families in this generation have failed miserably in that respect. In ancient China the people desired security from the barbaric hordes to the north, so they joined together to build the Great Wall. It was so high they knew no one could climb over it and so thick that nothing could break it down. Pleased with their accomplishment, they settled back to enjoy their security. During the first years of the Wall's existence, China was invaded several times. Not once did the barbaric hordes break down the Wall or climb over the top. Each time they bribed a gatekeeper and then marched right through the gate. The Chinese were so busy relying on their wall of stone that they forgot to teach integrity to their children, who grew up to guard the gates.

One Christian writer observed, "In His wisdom the Lord has decreed that the family shall be the greatest of all educational agencies" (*The Adventist Home*, p. 182).

How do we transfer values, define standards, teach integrity, and model acceptable behavior in our computer chip society? Rather than lament what the modern family has lost, it may be more profitable to take a creative look at what we have gained.

"In His wisdom the Lord has decreed that the family shall be the greatest of all educational agencies."

1. Shorter workweeks than our grandparents had mean more free time. What better way to spend that extra time than with our family?

2. Modern timesaving conveniences free us from many tasks that took hours or even days to perform a few generations ago. Invest the time saved with your family.

3. Modern transportation shortens the distance to grandma's house. We can be anywhere on the continent within a few hours. That includes the homes of grandparents and other extended family members.

4. VCRs and television provide instant entertainment and baby-sitting. Include some educational videos as a part of your regular viewing mix. Most libraries have an excellent supply of how-to and culturally enriching videos. Apply for a library card, and check out at least one video—or more—a week to watch and discuss with your family.

5. Satellites bring instant news from around the world right into our family rooms. Set aside a special news hour several times a week. Watch a newscast together, and then discuss with your family how God relates to us through everyday events. You will probably find that any children past the age of 6 will contribute eagerly to the discussion.

6. Visit your local religious bookstore, and browse through the vast array of home worship materials designed for families. Purchase a new idea and give it a try.

7. If you have teenagers in your family, try a music appreciation night. That means you (the parents) make an honest effort to learn to appreciate your teen's music. Listen to a song from one of his or her favorite albums, and ask for an explanation of what it means to him or her. Try to listen through your teen's ears. Then play one of your favorites, and explain what it means to you.

8. Spend one evening a month looking through picture albums, viewing slides, or watching videotapes of your family. This includes extended family as well. Follow a leisurely pace, but set a time limit. When a picture reminds any family member of a story, stop and relive the experience.

9. Make dinner an absolute family priority. With our modern conveniences a meal can go from the freezer to the table in 30 minutes or less. Make certain everyone understands the importance of this meal together. Make it a cooperative effort involving everyone. Parents must set the tone to prevent conflict. Make it clear that dinner isn't the appropriate time to unload grievances (this applies to parents also).

Some would say that Christian behavior and family values are more caught than taught. A Sunday school teacher asked a group of children, "Why do you believe in God?" In reporting some of the answers, the teacher confessed that the one she liked best came from a little boy who said, "I don't know, unless it's something that runs in the family."

Ozzie and Harriet may have left town, but the modern family—whatever its configuration—has more opportunities to share Christian values, define Christian standards, and model Christian behavior than any previous generation.

That is indeed good news!

Thought Questions

1. Think back on the family in which you were raised. What are your earliest memories?

2. Review Genesis 1 and 2, and write a brief description of "family" in the Garden of Eden.

3. How does the following statement relate to your family? "In His wisdom the Lord has decreed that the family shall be the greatest of all educational agencies" (*The Adventist Home*, p. 182).

CHAPTER 2

"You've Been Acting Like This Since the Day You Were Born!"

(Controlling Hereditary Tendencies)

> *"It will be well to remember that tendencies of character are transmitted from parents to children. . . . In the fear of God gird on the armor for a life conflict with hereditary tendencies"* (Ellen G. White, Testimonies for the Church, *vol. 4, p. 439).*

Robin Hawkins, of Grand Rapids, Michigan, racked up nearly $2,300 in damages in two months . . . and she's only 2 years old! Robin's tale of terror began at the toilet. Alice—the cat—got dunked, drowned, and flushed. Robin's father neatly tallied the expenses in a yellow tablet: $62.75 for the plumber and $2.50 for Alice.

Robin decided to give teddy bear a bath—atop the heating element in the dishwasher. It cost her father $375 for repairs, $25 for smoke damage, and, of course, $8 for the teddy bear.

The refrigerator was next. It seems that Robin stuck some magnetic letters in the vents just before the family left home for the weekend. As a result, the motor burned out. The cost: $310 for the refrigerator, $120 in spoiled food, and $3.75 for the magnetic letters.

One day Robin's mother went to pick up her husband from his second job as a part-time officer (probably necessitated by Robin's adventures). She left Robin sleeping in her safety seat, with the keys in her purse inside the car. Mother heard the car start up, and both parents ran outside just in time to watch the car head down the street. Robin ran the car into a tree. Cost: $1,029.52 in repairs.

In addition, Robin lifted $620 out of the cash register at a supermarket, drilled 50 holes in the walls of a rental property owned by her parents, painted walls with nail polish, and slipped the garden tractor out of gear so it rolled down the driveway and narrowly missed a neighbor out on a walk.

"Someday when she comes and asks me why she isn't getting any allowance, I'll show her this," her father yelled, waving the yellow pad containing his list of costs resulting from the damage Robin had caused.

Where did Robin get her tendencies to destroy property and fall into mischief? Did she learn them from her parents in two short years of life? According to an ongoing study at University of Minnesota, "heredity may be a stronger influence on some personality traits than child rearing or family environment" (*USA Today*, Dec. 3, 1986).

During the past decade Drs. Thomas Bouchard and David Lykken have studied identical twins (siblings from the same egg) in a effort to understand why people behave the way they do. In their research Drs. Bouchard and Lykken have reunited identical twins separated since birth. Most of the twins studied had been adopted shortly after birth and were unaware they even had an identical brother or sister. Each twin was given a battery of tests during a 10-day period. They answered 15,000 questions, and this information was analyzed by computer to determine similarities. The researchers found that identical twins raised in separate environments were often more alike than twins raised in the same home.

"Heredity may be a stronger influence on some personality traits than child rearing or family environment."

Case 1: Male identical twins, 39 years of age, separated at about 37 days. When they were 10 years old, both twins developed sinus headaches. By the time the twins reached their teens the headaches had become migraines. Both had a similar history of chest pain, with pain traveling into the left arm. Both described their pain in the same way and both were hospitalized for that condition. Other similarities included a nervous condition treated with Valium, woodworking as a hobby, volunteer work for a police agency, clerical jobs, and identical scores on occupational testing.

Case 2: Male identical twins, 24 years of age, separated at five days. Both twins were overweight until junior high school and then became extremely skinny. Both were overt and active homosexuals before meeting each other. Both developed a fear of heights during childhood but showed gradual improvement during their teen years and later. Both had speech problems in elementary school and were hyperactive in first grade.

Case 3: Female identical twins, 57 years of age, separated at about six weeks. When both twins became teenagers they had identical nightmares, which gradually stopped by the time the twins reached their mid-40s. They imagined doorknobs and fishhooks in their mouths and felt they were being smothered to death. In addition, they both wet the bed until they were 12 or 13, and they reported similar educational and marital histories.

Case 4: Female identical twins, 39 years of age, separated within two weeks of their birth. Nicknamed the "giggle sisters" because of their constant outbursts of identical, raucous laughter, both walked, talked, and dressed the same even though they had never met. Blue was their favorite color, and their personal libraries contained many of the same books—they both enjoyed reading family sagas in particular. From the first moment they met, one twin would begin a sentence and the other would finish it. Then both would laugh and say "Yes" in unison. Their houses are decorated with the same colors and with similar furniture, and both twins last moved in 1976.

An inspired mother and author made that same conclusion about 100 years ago: "Many children have received as a birthright almost unconquerable tendencies to evil" (*The Adventist Home*, p. 256). "Conflict after conflict must be waged against hereditary tendencies."

What does this tell us about heredity and our behavior? We are a product of both our genetic inheritance and our environment. Drs. Bouchard and Lykken estimate that most temperament tendencies are about 50 percent inherited and about 50 percent learned. The one tendency that seems to be mostly inherited is leadership.

Recent studies indicate that even the tendency toward criminal behavior may be inherited. James Wilson and Richard Herrnstein conclude, in their book *Crime and Human Nature*, that biological parents who are criminals tend to produce children who, even after adoption, display the same sorts of problems. Their conclusion is not that criminals are born, but that some children are born with a greater *disposition* to crime than others.

An inspired mother and author made that same conclusion about 100 years ago: "Many children have received as a birthright almost unconquerable tendencies to evil" (*The Adventist Home*, p. 256). "Conflict after conflict must be waged against hereditary tendencies" (Ellen G. White, *Christ's Object Lessons*, p. 331).

Scripture confirms that we have a twofold nature at birth. We are *conceived in sin* (Ps. 51:5) and yet are *designed by God* (Ps. 139:13-16).

An ancient Greek physician and philosopher, Hippocrates, understood human nature very well and even attempted to theorize the cause of behavior. Hippocrates postulated that temperament was determined by four basic body fluids: blood, yellow bile, black bile, and phlegm. According to his theory, the predominance of a particular fluid would determine one's temperament. The ancient words for these four body fluids are still used to describe temperament types today: *sanguine* (blood), *choleric* (yellow bile), *melancholy* (black bile), and *phlegmatic* (phlegm).

Experts in genetics tell us that there are about 280 billion chromosome combinations possible per couple. Therefore, the likelihood of two individuals being exactly identical are about one in 300 billion.

Even though modern researchers would refer to hormones or DNA rather than body fluids as a determining factor for temperament, the original words that Hippocrates settled on are still widely used.

Before examining these four temperament types, I would offer a word of caution. None of us is a single temperament. We are all blends. Experts in genetics tell us that there are about 280 billion chromosome combinations possible per couple. Therefore, the likelihood of two individuals being exactly identical are about one in 300 billion. However, that should not discourage us from looking for common tendencies that are easily identifiable in our children. It's easier than you might think.

Sanguine

Sanguine children are *emotional extroverts*, who enjoy life *now*. They are friendly, talkative, and lovable. Their winning smile prevents many scoldings and may even make us laugh in spite of our anger.

My wife and I met a typical sanguine child at Disney World some years ago. He ran up to us, with his parents about 10 steps behind. "Say, mister," he asked excitedly, "can I look at your program?"

I smiled and handed him my directory.

He began to compare my leaflet with his and then turned to his parents with a big smile, "See, Dad! I told you mine was different from anyone else's." With that he handed back my program and headed for another lucky tourist.

Both parents looked at us, smiled, shrugged their shoulders, and took off after their sanguine son.

These outgoing children are likely to be loud and boisterous and will learn to cover up mistakes early in life.

A sanguine little girl was looking at books in the school library when in walked the superintendent of schools. The librarian and older students were terribly flustered since they knew him to be a no-nonsense individual. They held their breath as he sat down beside the little girl to assist her with a pre-primer. The book consisted of single items on a page with the proper descriptive word at the bottom. He asked the little tyke to identify the items.

As he turned the pages she responded gleefully, "That's a boy. A girl. A house. A car. A top. A truck."

She was doing just great until he came to a picture of a hatchet. "That's a hammer!" she responded enthusiastically.

The superintendent did not say a word as he turned the page. There was a hammer. The little girl grabbed the book, looked at the hammer, turned back to the hatchet, then back to the hammer. She quickly closed the book and, smiling sweetly, announced, "Sir, we are in the library, and we really shouldn't be talking like this!"

Sanguine children usually have a very short attention span. If they get a new toy, it will be the center of their attention for five minutes maximum. Whether it is a toy, a book, a TV program, homework, or church, they find it difficult to stay interested. Because of their short attention span, they are seldom good students.

Besides being reckless and undisciplined, they have a weak will that seems to keep them constantly in hot water. They are also impulsive show-offs and clowns. During their early years we find this amusing. Later it becomes irritating and embarrassing.

Fortunately, sanguines quickly forget past punishment and never seem to hold a grudge. Although they complain loudly while discipline is being administered, they will forget all about it five minutes later.

Sanguine children do not like to play alone, and they quickly learn to share their possessions. They find early in life that sharing is an excellent way to make new friends. Even though they often have a quick temper, it is short-lived. Almost as soon as they flare up in anger, sanguines will apologize and want to make things right. "I'm sorry, I didn't mean to" is a frequently used phrase in their vocabulary.

Sanguine children need lots of love and acceptance at home. If their parents quarrel, they take it personally and sometimes withdraw into a shell. However, if their parents teach them spiritual things, no one is more receptive or responsive.

Of all the temperaments, the sanguine is the easiest to mold.

Sanguine children usually have a very short attention span. If they get a new toy, it will be the center of their attention for five minutes maximum. Because of their short attention span, they are seldom good students.

Choleric

Choleric children are *unemotional extroverts*, who seem to live in the future. Almost from early childhood cholerics begin to plan their lives. They are take-charge people, and their temperament is perhaps the easiest to discern at an early age. I have had parents diagnose a choleric child before the infant is a year old. The independent spirit and self-sufficient nature is easily observable.

One parent of a choleric child asked, "Did you get homesick while you were away at summer camp?"

"No, not me!" responded choleric Jimmy, "but some of the kids were who had dogs."

Cholerics seem to be born manipulators. They learn very early that withholding something often gives them a bargaining edge. I remember reading about little Benjamin, who sat down to write a letter to God asking for a baby sister.

Benny started out the letter: "Dear God, I've been a good boy." He paused, thought for a moment, then commented, "No, God won't believe that."

He wadded up the paper, threw it away, and started again. "Dear God, Most of the time I've been a good boy." He stopped again, thinking, *God won't be moved by this.* Into the trash can went the wadded up paper.

Ben thought for a few moments, jumped up, and ran to the bathroom. He grabbed a big towel, brought it into the living room, and laid it on the couch. Going to the fireplace, he reached up and removed a statue of the virgin Mary that he had eyed many times.

He placed the statue in the middle of the towel, gently folded over the edges, and placed a rubber band around the whole thing. He brought it to the table, took another piece of paper, and began writing his third letter to God. He started with: "Dear God, If You ever want to see Your mother again . . ."

A manipulative spirit combined with a strong will makes choleric children rather difficult to discipline or nurture. James Dobson has written a book that I recommend for parents of choleric children—*The Strong-willed Child.* In another chapter we will discuss some discipline techniques that may prove valuable for parents of choleric children.

A manipulative spirit combined with a strong will makes choleric children rather difficult to discipline or nurture.

Cholerics are very active and are usually neighborhood leaders. If other choleric children are in the neighborhood, there may likely be confrontations. Cholerics are usually blunt, sarcastic, and even brutal in their honesty. They speak what they think without giving thought to the consequences.

One day my wife was baby-sitting a choleric child from next door, and he told her, "I don't have to mind you. You're not my mother!"

Fortunately, I was close enough to hear the challenge and quickly made him understand that even though we were not his parents, he would behave. Once I established that fact, we had no more trouble.

Perhaps a parent's hardest task will be *not* to take the outbursts from choleric children personally—to accept the confrontation, channel their wills, and preserve their spirits.

Choleric children usually mature earlier than children with one of the other temperaments. Most need well-defined areas of responsibility and leadership at an early age. In addition, they often decide for baptism earlier than their peers.

We should not ignore their decision. I have counseled with many heartbroken parents who deeply regret not allowing their choleric children to be baptized when they requested it. The older that choleric children become without the Lord, the less likely they are ever to accept Him. Their self-sufficient nature soon teaches them that they can get along without their parents, without their teachers, and without God. It is far better to baptize such children when they want to accept Jesus, rather than when we think they are old enough.

Melancholy

Melancholy children are *emotional introverts*, who tend to spend a great deal of time reflecting on the past—especially past mistakes. They are usually very gifted and yet feel insecure. Anything less than an A on a report card they consider failing. They often sulk for days or go into deep periods of depression, only to bounce back unexplainably and become almost hyperactive the following week. Their sensitive nature is greatly affected by what others think or say about them—especially are they affected by those they care about or love.

Billy was attending his first day at junior high school. The day began with an assembly that featured the introduction of all the homeroom teachers. First to be introduced was Miss Smith, and the ninth graders, knowing Miss Smith to be an easy grader and not much of a disciplinarian, all began to cheer, "Yea, Miss Smith! Right on, Miss Smith!"

The next person to be introduced was Mr. Brown, who was a young and popular teacher and a special favorite of the students. This time, the eighth graders joined in with thundering approval. "Yea, Mr. Brown! Hurray for Mr. Brown!"

By the time the next teacher was introduced, even the seventh graders were getting into the spirit of things. Then Mr. Johnson, an older teacher who was reputed to be the hardest grader and the least sympathetic teacher in the school, was introduced. In addition, Mr. Johnson lived right down the block from Billy. The catcalls began, "Boo, Mr. Johnson! Hiss, hiss! Boo, Mr. Johnson!" The pain was evident on old Mr. Johnson's face.

Suddenly Billy jumped up in the middle of the bleachers and shouted, "Shut up! He's my father!"

The noise instantly died down as the word was passed. "Hey, cool it! Johnson's son is here."

That afternoon when school was out, Billy raced home as fast as he could, and as he went through the front door, he was sobbing. His father met him and asked, "Son, what's wrong?"

"Daddy, I've got to talk to you. I told a lie in school today."

"Better tell me about it, son."

Parents of melancholy children need to understand their children's sensitivity. Melancholies cannot handle criticism and are easily wounded.

So Billy told the story. When he was through, his father put his arms around him. "It's all right, son. You didn't really tell a lie; you just got your family members mixed up. Mr. Johnson's not your father—he's your brother."

Parents of melancholy children need to understand their children's sensitivity. Melancholies cannot handle criticism and are easily wounded. Telling a lie can be devastating. But watching a friend being ridiculed is also devastating. Teaching children about truth and integrity, while being sensitive to their temperament, is often a difficult task for parents of melancholy children.

Melancholies are true friends and remain bonded for life. While they do not make friends easily, they remain faithful to the friends they make. If they do not have a close confidant when they are young, they often escape into a fantasy world with "imaginary" friends.

Phlegmatic

Phlegmatic children are *unemotional introverts*, who are naturally quiet and easygoing. As babies they seldom fuss, and they make their parents look great as child trainers. Unlike active sanguines and cholerics, phleg-matic children seem to be contented wherever they are located. If you take them to church, they will not fuss or embarrass you. If you take them to a restaurant, they peacefully watch the diners and thoroughly enjoy them-selves. They are seldom demanding and are usually contented. They are born spectators and thoroughly enjoy people-watching. As they grow older, they seem to want to please adults or anyone in a position of authority.

The story is told about a phlegmatic little boy who answered the telephone at home. The caller was a salesman who asked, "Is your mother home?"

"No."

"Is your father at home?"

Once again the boy replied, "No."

Finally the frustrated salesman asked, "Is there anyone else at home I can speak to?"

"Yes. My sister is here."

"Fine," the salesman sighed, "can I speak with her?"

"OK," the boy responded. This was followed by a long pause. Finally, the little boy returned. "I'm back," he announced.

"Where's your sister?" shouted the frustrated salesman.

"I can't lift her out of the playpen."

Phlegmatic children seem to be ideal offspring when they're young. Whatever their parents ask them to do, they comply without question. Except when it comes to eating. Phlegmatics are usually very slow eaters. This makes an interesting test of wills when the parent is a sanguine or choleric, both of whom traditionally eat very rapidly.

Our choleric neighbor invited us for dinner, and her phlegmatic little son sat in his high chair by her side. When we had finished the first course, he had barely touched his food. She began to harangue him, "You will sit right there until you eat every bite on your plate!"

Smiling sweetly, he responded, "OK."

With that she continued, "You won't get any dessert until you've cleaned your plate!"

Continuing to smile sweetly, he agreed, "OK."

After a few more rounds of "OK," she was ready to climb the walls. She expected her phlegmatic son to eat as rapidly as she, which created a stressful situation for herself as she tried to motivate him to eat like a choleric.

Phlegmatic children do have a tendency to be selfish. One interesting way to tell a sanguine and a phlegmatic apart is by what they do with their toys. If the doorbell rings and the neighborhood kids are coming over to play, a sanguine child runs to the door with an armload of toys, passing them out as the other kids enter the house. A phlegmatic child puts all the toys away first and stuffs the last one under his or her sweatshirt just before opening the door. Our task as parents is to discern our children's predominant temperament traits and relate to them accordingly. The book *Child Guidance* offers the following counsel and assurance:

"Marked diversities of disposition and character frequently exist in the same family, for it is in the order of God that persons of varied temperament should associate together. When this is the case, each member of the household should sacredly regard the feelings and respect the right of the others. By this means mutual consideration and forbearance will be cultivated, prejudices will be softened, and rough points of character smoothed. Harmony may be secured, and the blending of the varied temperaments may be a benefit to each."

"Marked diversities of disposition and character frequently exist in the same family, for it is in the order of God that persons of varied temperament should associate together. When this is the case, each member of the household should sacredly regard the feelings and respect the right of the others. By this means mutual consideration and forbearance will be cultivated, prejudices will be softened, and rough points of character smoothed. Harmony may be secured, and the blending of the varied temperaments may be a benefit to each" (p. 205).

As we attempt to understand our children's temperament blends, it would be well for us to consider our own. How do we react under stress? What temperament characteristics do we possess? How do these traits affect our relationship with others, including our children? How do we discipline our children? How consistent are we? Perhaps you may want to a take a moment to review the temperament chart on page 40.

Notice that each temperament has its own set of strengths and weaknesses. You will get a more accurate picture of your unique blend if you cross out everything on the chart that does not apply to you; circle everything on the chart that applies to you occasionally; and then carefully note all the unmarked strengths and weaknesses you display most of the time. If this seems shocking to you, just remember that your friends, relatives, and other family members have known this about you for years. So relax, and focus on the positive.

Sanguine parents often spend a great deal of time issuing warning tickets. I have often wished I could be stopped by a sanguine police officer so I could get off with a warning! With the warning from sanguine parents comes a threat that is not immediately carried out. Eventually sanguine parents' anger button is pushed, and they explode. After the explosive anger has worn off, they will feel very guilty and usually try to patch things up. Sanguine parents are very inconsistent with discipline. How much children will get away with depends a great deal on the mood of sanguine parents.

Choleric parents are usually the most forceful. When choleric parents give a command, they expect it to be carried out—*immediately*.

My mother used to give me warning after warning, but I knew from experience just about how long I could wait before I actually had to comply (although occasionally I would miscalculate and experience her wrath). We lived on a dairy farm, and she would help Dad milk the cows in the morning. When it was time for us kids to get ready for school, she would return to the house and awaken us. Before she left for the barn again she wanted to hear us moving upstairs. So I would lean over the bed and rattle my shoes around on the floor, then go back to sleep. I knew I did not really have to get up until she said, "If you don't get down here right now, I'm coming up there with a switch!" That was my clue to comply instantly. That clue usually came on her third trip back from the barn. I have often thought how much time she could have saved us both if she had meant what she said the first time.

Choleric parents are usually the most forceful. When choleric parents give a command, they expect it to be carried out—*immediately*. Choleric parents usually give one warning . . . and then comes their wrath. Choleric parents do not make idle threats. Discipline is consistent, but usually without love. This style of training can devastate melancholy children.

The teacher was asking her students what each wanted to become when he or she grew up. She received a variety of interesting answers such as president, fire fighter, teacher, etc. But the one that caught her attention came from Melancholy Mary, who responded, "I want to be possible!"

"Possible?" asked the teacher.

"Yes," replied Mary. "Mommy is always telling me that I'm impossible, so when I grow up I want to be *possible*!"

Melancholy parents tend to blame themselves for their children's bad behavior and often read into their youngster's actions more than was intended. "Where did I go wrong?" they frequently lament, meant to elicit both sympathy and compliance. They tend to talk and lecture a great deal, while saving actual hands-on discipline as a last resort.

> **Melancholy parents tend to blame themselves for their children's bad behavior and often read into their youngster's actions more than was intended.**

A child of melancholy parents remarked, "I'm really worried. Dad slaves away at his job so I'll never want for anything and will be able to go to the university when I get older. Mom works hard every day washing and ironing, cleaning up after me, taking care of me when I get sick. They spend every day of their lives working just on my behalf. I'm worried."

His little friend inquired, "What have you got to worry about?"

"I'm afraid they might try to escape," admitted the child.

Phlegmatic parents tend to retreat from discipline and hope someone else will be the "heavy." Usually a phlegmatic parent is married to a choleric or sanguine, who will provide the needed guidance. Phlegmatic parents tend to ignore misbehavior and tune out problems. This makes them very unpopular for home visitation. While phlegmatic parents sit sipping a hot drink with you, their children are tearing your house apart, while they seem oblivious to the entire situation. Occasionally, if things get really bad, phlegmatic parents will say, "You just wait until your father [mother] gets back. Then you'll get it good!"

My wife is melancholy/phlegmatic and does not like to be the "heavy" when discipline is necessary. One day when we were visiting my folks on the farm, she and our son had a misunderstanding. I was with my dad in the barn, and she told our son, "You sit right there in that corner until your father comes back."

I was completely unaware that she was having any problems, so when Dad and I finished the chores, we hopped into his truck and went to town. To this day my wife does not remember how she finally got our son out of the corner, but she does remember it as a very uncomfortable situation.

Understanding our own temperament blends helps us relate to our children when discipline is necessary.

Sanguine children will protest the loudest and resent our controlling their actions. No one wants more freedom than sanguines. They will spout off about how unreasonable we are being as they cry and stomp their feet. Improper discipline methods can result in rebellious sanguine children. This rebellion may go relatively unnoticed until their teen years, when all their resentment will come pouring forth as they attempt to break free of their "restrictive" nest.

Choleric children will display better control over their outward emotions than sanguines do, but inwardly they may become bitter and stubborn over what they feel is unreasonable discipline. Cholerics have this inner need to "get even" when they have been injured either physically or psychologically. If we do not establish "justice" in a given situation, they will often take the law into their own hands.

Jack's mother heard loud screams coming from the playroom. She ran into the room to find 2-year-old Sissy with both hands in Jack's hair, pulling as hard as she could.

Mother gently released the little girl's grip and said comfortingly to Jack, "There, there. Sissy didn't mean it. She doesn't know that hurts."

Mother had just barely left the room when she heard Sissy scream. Rushing back into the room, she asked, "What happened?"

With a satisfied smile on his face, Jack replied, "She knows now!"

Melancholy children appear to conform to discipline, but inwardly are often seething with hostility. Like cholerics, melancholies want to get even, but they seldom dare. Instead, they spend a great deal of time recalling the incident and reliving it again and again. Because each recollection reinforces the belief that they have been dealt with unfairly, they may grow up narrow-minded, self-righteous, and outwardly pious, but inside they may be filled with hostility and unresolved anger. Parents should never forget the sensitive nature of melancholy children, who are easily hurt by the most innocent remark. It requires a great deal of self-control and tact to discipline such children.

"There are some children who need more patient discipline and kindly training than others. They have received a legacy of unpromising traits of character, and because of this they need the more of sympathy and love. . . . They may possess undeveloped powers which, when aroused, will enable them to fill places far in advance of those from whom more has been expected. . . . If you have children with peculiar temperaments, do not, because of this, let the blight of discouragement rest upon their lives. . . . Strengthen them by loving words and kindly deeds to overcome their defects of character" (Ellen G. White, *Counsels to Parents and Teachers*, pp. 115, 116).

If you have children with peculiar temperaments, do not, because of this, let the blight of discouragement rest upon their lives. . . . Strengthen them by loving words and kindly deeds to overcome their defects of character."

Phlegmatic children may appear to be the easiest to discipline because of their immediate compliance. However, strict discipline may actually prevent them from maturing. Their quiet, passive, fearful compliance may make life easier for us now, but infinitely more difficult when we try to encourage phlegmatic children to leave the nest. Severe discipline may make phlegmatic children so dependent upon our decision-making that they will never have the courage to venture out into the adult world. They need encouragement to be more assertive; we should not try to break their will.

Scripture offers a promise that for some parents seems more like a curse: "Train a child in the way he should go, and when he is old he will not turn from it" (Prov. 22:6, NIV). But what about children who rebel during their teen years? What about children who reject your religious beliefs? What about children who don't seem to respond to your training? Does that mean that as a parent you have failed God?

I cannot begin to count the number of guilt-ridden parents I have counseled during the past 15 years who have worried that somehow they have failed God because their children have not responded to spiritual matters.

The Hebrew word translated "train" has several meanings. It can refer to the mouth, gum, or palate area inside the mouth. In some contexts it might apply to a bit or bridle being placed in the mouth of an untamed horse. The New Testament explains this concept clearly: "If we put bits into the mouths of horses that they may obey us, we guide their whole bodies" (James 3:3, RSV). In this sense it refers to training in the same manner you would domesticate an animal. It does not mean "to reason with" or "discuss the possibilities." It means to direct with a firm hand. At this point, it has nothing to do with the power of choice.

My wife, Karen, once took our son's German shepherd to obedience school in the evenings. Since I was pastoring, it was not possible for me to attend the night sessions. She complained that she was having difficulty getting Smokey (our dog) to comply. All he wanted to do was lick her hand and jump up on her. However, each morning I took Smokey jogging with me, and when we returned I would go through the hand and voice signals with him. Smokey performed perfectly every morning. Yet when Karen took him to obedience school, he still would not obey.

As we analyzed the problem, it became apparent that Smokey simply did not believe that Karen was in command. Her voice is so soft and sweet that it did not carry enough authority. Melancholy and phlegmatic parents often experience the same difficulty training their children.

In Arabic the same root verb translated "train" also refers to the practice of putting date syrup in a newborn's mouth to make certain the child will have the sucking instinct necessary for survival. The sweet taste creates a thirst for mother's milk, which means life to the child. Likewise, parents should create in their children a thirst for living water. Such thirst is best accomplished in an atmosphere of love and respect rather than one of fear and resentment.

Proverbs next refers to a "child." How old should children be before we stop their training? This Hebrew word refers to a newly born infant (1 Sam.

4:21), as well as a son who does not yet know right from wrong (Isa. 7:16), often felt by the Hebrews to be the age of 12. In other words, it covers the entire span from birth until the child is old enough to make wise decisions on his or her own.

"In the way he should go" can be literally translated "in accordance to the way [he was designed by God]." Parents should remember that each child is unique. Each child bears the design of God. If we are truly to discover how God designed our children, we must discover their temperament blends. We must become familiar with our children's strengths and weaknesses. God does not make clones. He is a lover of the unique. Therefore, we cannot train every child the same. Each child responds according to his or her own temperament blend. We cannot train a sanguine using the same techniques we would use for a phlegmatic. Children must be trained in the way God designed them to function—in ways appropriate to their age as well as their temperament.

"We all need to study character and manner that we may know how to deal judiciously with different minds, that we may use our best endeavors to help them to a correct understanding of the word of God and to a true Christian life.

"We all need to study character and manner that we may know how to deal judiciously with different minds, that we may use our best endeavors to help them to a correct understanding of the word of God and to a true Christian life. . . . The person must be shown his true character, understand his own peculiarities of disposition and temperament, and see his infirmities" (*Testimonies*, vol. 4, p. 69).

"When he is old" refers to old age. The root word is the noun "beard," but the adjective can refer to both men and women. In the Old Testament it always refers to the elderly—such as Abraham when he was 99 and Sarah when she was 89 or 90 (Gen. 18).

"He will not turn from it" has probably caused more grief to parents than any other clause in the Bible. Some parents feel that they have successfully fulfilled this verse when their children remain faithful church members. Others feel like a failure because their children choose to quit attending the church of their parents. Just what is the "it" that this text refers to?

"It" might refer to the training the child received during his or her growing years. Studies indicate that we never fully outgrow our childhood training or experiences. What we were taught (or caught) during childhood stays with us for a lifetime. One author suggests that though we date the adult, we marry the child! So "it" may logically apply to childhood training and experiences.

However, "it" could also refer to "the way he should go." In other words, the way designed by God or the appropriate way that is in keeping with the individual's age and temperament.

I would suggest that we cannot really separate the two meanings. If you are truly going to train your children, it must be in accordance with the way they were designed by God.

How am I training my children? Am I taking the time to discern how God designed them? Am I teaching them according to their temperament blends or mine? Am I parenting according to my comfort level or theirs? Am I training them daily to understand the strengths God placed within them and to thank God for them? Have I made them aware that their weaknesses are part of their genetic inheritance and not just a learned behavior? Do I spend most of my time complimenting them on God's design or reminding them of sin's inheritance? Have I shared with them the power of the cross and God's forgiveness? Have I helped them understand that "if we confess our sins to him, he can be depended on to forgive us and to cleanse us from every wrong. [And it is perfectly proper for God to do this for us because Christ died to wash away our sins]" (1 John 1:9, TLB)?

Has my training been consistent from the cradle to the altar? Have I truly taken the time to understand my children's needs? Do I fully understand that they, too, have the power of choice and will one day exercise that power? Will I support them as they make those decisions?

Sometimes the cause of parental distress is our inability to "read" our children's temperaments. Once we understand that our children were designed by God, we can claim the power of the Holy Spirit in our training sessions, because we understand God's blueprint. But we must not judge the effectiveness of our training by the happiness of our children. If we happen to have sanguine or phlegmatic children, they will probably be happy most of the time. If they are choleric or melancholy, happiness may not be high on their list of priorities.

The most important challenge for parents is not merely to create happiness, but to teach *responsibility*. The real work of parenting is to train children to be responsible for their own decisions as they venture out into the world.

The message of Proverbs 22:6 is this: Train up a child from infancy in accordance with the temperament blend given to him by God, and when that child is mature he or she will take full responsibility for his or her own life.

Sometimes the cause of parental distress is our inability to "read" our children's temperaments. Once we understand that our children were designed by God, we can claim the power of the Holy Spirit in our training sessions, because we understand God's blueprint.

Thought Questions

1. How does the following statement relate to your family? "It will be well to remember that tendencies of character are transmitted from parents to children. . . . In the fear of God gird on the armor for a life conflict with hereditary tendencies" (*Testimonies*, vol. 4, p. 439).

2. What is your temperament blend, and how does it affect your parenting style?

3. Reflect on this verse and your personal experience: "Train a child in the way he should go, and when he is old he will not turn from it" (Prov. 22:6, NIV).

TYPICAL CAREERS
Public Speaker
Actor or Actress
Salesperson
Preacher
Receptionist
Courtroom Lawyer
Public Relations

TYPICAL CAREERS
Manager
Builder/Contractor
Promoter
Executor
President
Crusader
Producer

EXTROVERT

TIME REFERENCE
Present

TIME REFERENCE
Future

Share people's joys and sorrows, stimulating, personable, enthusiastic, ambitious, compassionate, dramatic, outgoing, cheerful, friendly, sincere, warm, sociable, talkative, happy, carefree, easy to apologize, makes good first impression.

Strong-willed, adventuresome, determined, time efficient, independent, perceptive, visionary, energetic, optimistic, productive, decisive, courageous, leader, practical, organized, self-confident.

← STRENGTHS →

← WEAKNESSES →

EMOTIONAL

UNEMOTIONAL

Disorganized, undisciplined, unproductive, restless, excitable, weak-willed, loud, egotistical, self-centered, undependable, exaggerates, fearful, indecisive, distractable.

Crafty, self-sufficient, unsympathetic, impetuous, proud, domineering, sarcastic, inconsiderate, unforgiving, highly opinionated, unpredictive, aggressive, hard to please.

SANGUINE

CHOLERIC

MELANCHOLY

PHLEGMATIC

Moody, negative, rigid, conforming, unsure, ingratiating, dependent, awkward, touchy, pessimistic, self-centered, revengeful, unsociable, persecution-prone, critical, depression, impractical, emotional.

Stubborn, indulgent, resentful, blasé, unmotivated, spectator, uninvolved, conforming, unsure, ingratiating, dependent, awkward, self-protective, selfish, slow, indecisive, fearful, tease, lazy.

Precise, gifted, analytical, persistent, industrious, serious, exacting, orderly, sensitive, perfectionist, conscientious, loyal, idealistic, theoretical, self-sacrificing, creative, self-disciplined, knows own limitations.

Calm, quiet, easy-going, flexible, practical, leader, supportive, likeable, willing, diplomatic, dependable, humorous, agreeable, kind-hearted, efficient, peace-loving, tactful, conservative, works well under pressure, neat, organized, objective, attentive.

← WEAKNESSES →

← STRENGTHS →

TIME REFERENCE
Past

TIME REFERENCE
Spectator

TYPICAL CAREERS
Interior Decorator
Fashion Designer
Author
Professor
Philosopher
Physician or Nurse
Musician

INTROVERT

TYPICAL CAREERS
Accountant
Technician
Diplomat
Teacher
Counselor
Administrator

CHAPTER 3

"Why Can't You Behave Like Your Brother/Sister?"

(The Family "Pecking Order")

> "Visiting the iniquity of the fathers upon the children and the children's children, to the third and fourth generation" (Ex. 34:7, RSV).

Two small boys walked into the dentist's office. The older boy spoke bravely, "I want a tooth taken out, and I don't want any gas, and I don't want it deadened—because we're in a hurry!"

"You're a brave young man," beamed the dentist. "Which tooth is it?"

Turning to his younger brother, the boy replied, "Show him your tooth, Albert."

A recent study indicates that genetics shapes the personality three to five times more than does the home environment. In fact, Dr. Robert Plomin of Pennsylvania State University states that home training accounts for less than 10 percent of the total behavior patterns. Plomin and his colleagues tracked a sample of 99 identical twins and 229 fraternal twins who were reared apart. They matched this sample against 160 identical twins and 212 fraternal twins who were raised together in the same home. The average age of both samples was 59, and it is the largest study of its kind. Here are some of the findings.

1. Those raised in *restrictive* homes tended to have their personalities molded more by the parents and less by genetics. As expected, those raised in *permissive* homes were the most likely to reveal inherited tendencies and qualities.

2. Even though children grow up in the same home, they do not experience the same environment.

This study seems to confirm that domineering parents shape the personality (and lives) of their children more than permissive parents do. However, it also revealed that children from restrictive/domineering families were more likely to have problems with social skills and acceptance. Apparently parents need to allow their children the freedom to discover who they are, while at the same time offering the security of boundaries. Combining this with a knowledge of social skills will prepare children to enter the adult world with confidence. (See *USA Today*, January 11, 1989.)

One factor not studied by Plomin was the birth order of the twins as they related to other siblings in their natural or adopted families. Dr. Kevin Leman has written an informative book on this subject, and he divides siblings into three categories: firstborn, middle child, and lastborn (Kevin Leman, *The Birth Order Book*).

While the exact percentage of home influence upon behavior patterns is open to debate, most would agree that it does play an important role in establishing values and social skills. It may even be an important factor in creating dysfunctional behavior patterns at a very early age. Therefore, understanding the family "pecking order" can be helpful to any parent concerned about the molding process.

The Leader (Firstborn)

Typical characteristics of firstborns include being perfectionistic, conscientious, list-makers, well organized, goal oriented, self-sacrificing, and reliable leaders. New parents expect a great deal from their first child—as well as from themselves. Since everything is for the first time, it becomes terribly important. The baby shower, nursery wallpaper, child's clothes, name selection, and even the establishment of a college fund are all important events for the new parents. Encyclopedia salespersons find these new parents easy prey and often sell them an encyclopedia set that will be outdated before junior learns to read. Even grandparents get caught up in the momentous occasion and tend to overdo for the firstborn. Consequently, this new branch on the family tree becomes the leader and standard-bearer for the family.

Research indicates that firstborns walk and talk earlier than their siblings—and is it any wonder with every adult in the family hanging on the firstborn's every "goo"? Perhaps firstborns learn to walk earlier in order to put distance between themselves and the constant adult prodding. Since firstborns have only adults as role models, it seems logical that they pick up adult behavior. With no other siblings to challenge their authority, firstborns assume that control is their God-given right.

A confident firstborn joined the other children at the front of the church for the children's story. The pastor announced that he was going to tell a story about frogs. Easing his way into the presentation, the pastor inquired, "When I say the word 'frog,' what's the first thing that comes to your mind?"

"God!" exclaimed the firstborn excitedly.

Firstborns develop confidence at an early age. As a result, these confident children are often called upon to be baby-sitter and even surrogate parent for their younger siblings. It is almost as if they never have an opportunity to be children themselves.

"Why do you think about God when I say 'frog'?" the surprised pastor inquired with obvious puzzlement.

"Because I know you didn't bring us down here to talk about frogs," the firstborn replied confidently.

Firstborns develop confidence at an early age. As a result, these confident children are often called upon to be baby-sitter and even surrogate parent for their younger siblings. It is almost as if they never have an opportunity to be children themselves. Perhaps that explains why 52 percent of all U.S. presidents and an even larger percentage of corporate executives are firstborns. They are natural leaders.

However, not all firstborns exhibit the same degree of leadership. Other factors such as inherited temperament blend, parental discipline style, culture, and peer group all play a role in determining behavior. Leman suggests that there are at least two types of firstborns: *compliant* and *strong-willed*. Compliant firstborns are often viewed as model children. Besides being conscientious and reliable, they utter such reassuring phrases as "Yes, Dad!" "Yes, Mom!" and "Thank you!" Compliant firstborns have a strong need for approval and become good students or workers.

My wife, Karen, is a compliant firstborn. Actually she is an only child. I am a strong-willed firstborn. Our temperaments and behavior patterns are opposite, yet we both display firstborn tendencies. When we eat at a restaurant and the food is cold or poorly prepared, I ask for a replacement. This embarrasses my wife, who would rather eat cold food than create a scene.

Strong-willed firstborns need to be the center of attraction even before leaving the womb. They are the classic type A personalities and begin making their desires known with frequent kicks and turns before they are born. Later they often become workaholics, addicted to the adrenaline of their hard-driving personalities. Even personal ads become obvious when written by firstborns.

"Christian, blonde, blue eyes, 5'2", 100 lbs., prof., cauc/female, no dependents, wishes to meet Protestant Christian, prof. man in 30s with college degree who has compassion for animals and people, loves nature, exercise, and phy. fitness (no team sports), music and dance, church and home life. Desire nonsmoker/nondrinker, slender, 5'7" -6', lots of head hair, no chest hair, intelligent, honest and trustworthy, sense of humor, excellent communicator of feelings, very sensitive, gentle, affectionate, androgynous attitude about roles, giving, encouraging, and helpful to others, no temper or ego problems, secure within and financially, health-conscious, neat and clean, extremely considerate and dependable. I believe in old-fashioned morals and values. If you do too and are interested in a possible Christian commitment, write to P.O. Box 82533. Please include recent color photo and address."

Isn't it interesting how perfectionism can narrow one's vision? Perhaps the writer of that ad would be better off reading the latest edition of *Grimm's Fairy Tales*!

A friend of mine once made a fortune establishing a company from virtually nothing. He operated out of his home for years and eventually sold the business for several million dollars. Yet even after becoming a millionaire, he seldom took time to enjoy his financial success.

Workaholics are goal-oriented and thrive on the next challenge. However, their addiction to making decisions and always being right makes it difficult for them to accept rejection or criticism. Apparently these very traits, pushed to their extreme, prompted the firstborn Cain to eventually murder his younger brother. Jesus reminds us that murder comes in many forms and can be performed with the tongue as well as with a knife. Many firstborns practice murder with their tongue.

Leman states that the majority of people in counseling are firstborns—frustrated and ridden with guilt. What can we as parents do to relieve some of the pressure on our firstborn children? Perhaps the most important thing we can do is *back off!* We should give our firstborns some room, enjoying this gift from God without making them into miniature adults. We can allow firstborns to be less than perfect. We should teach them how to laugh at their mistakes—and try again.

If you have a strong-willed firstborn, you may need help in establishing territorial boundaries. Unless you establish yourself as the authority figure early on in the relationship, you will probably lose all control of the child by the time he or she enters puberty. In addition to recommending Dr. James Dobson's excellent book *The Strong-willed Child*, I highly recommend Kay Kuzma's book *Building Your Child's Character From the Inside Out*, which I think should be required reading for every first-time parent.

If you have a strong-willed firstborn, you may need help in establishing territorial boundaries. Unless you establish yourself as the authority figure early on in the relationship, you will probably lose all control of the child by the time he or she enters puberty.

It is important for parents to teach firstborns to say "I'm sorry!" These words do not come easily to the proud, in-charge firstborns. Once they have mastered this phrase in both word and intent, we should teach them the companion phrase "Will you please forgive me?" We need to help our firstborns understand that it is OK to be imperfect, but it is not OK to be rude or impolite. Often firstborns will develop a view of God as a stern enforcer of laws who is unable to accept anyone who is not perfect. Since the only view of God young children have is through the actions of their parents, we should begin now to practice unconditional love with our firstborns and teach them to share such acceptance with others.

The Negotiator (Middle Child)

Lucy had set up her psychiatric advice booth from which she offered advice for a nickel. Charlie Brown inquired, "Lucy, I need help."

"What can I do for you, Charlie Brown?" she replied.

"I'm confused," continued Charlie. "I can't seem to find a direction, a purpose for life."

"Oh, don't worry, Charlie Brown. It's like being on a big ocean liner making its way through the sea. Some folks position their deck chairs to face the bow of the ship, and others place their chairs to face the side of the ship or the back of the ship. Which way do you face, Charlie Brown?"

Sadly Charlie responded, "I can't even unfold the deck chair."

Middle children are born into a dilemma. Just about the time they get used to being the youngest child, someone else takes over that coveted position. Middle children are born too late to get all the privileges and special attention offered firstborns, and they are born too soon to enjoy the relaxed discipline afforded lastborns.

Middle children often exhibit the *branching-off effect*. If the older sibling is more intelligent in a certain area, middle children will branch off in a different direction. If middle children are one of many children, they will look to the directions already pursued by those older but usually take a different route. While all siblings play off the firstborn, they also must be concerned about all others who are older in the family. This can have a dramatic effect on how they portray their natural temperament blends. If their temperament blends conflict with a role already taken, they may choose to suppress their natural inclinations so that they can be different.

It may be said that middle children get no respect. They are the Rodney

Dangerfields of siblings. Typical family photo albums have three times as many pictures of the first- or lastborns as those of middle children.

One 13-year-old middle child had just fallen into puppy love with the boy next door. She went to the family album to find a picture, and eventually yelled at her mother in frustration, "Aren't there any pictures of *me* without *her*?"

Friends often become the extended family of middle children because middle children do not hold the coveted first- or last-place position among siblings. To obtain reward and recognition, middle children turn to friends. (Firstborns typically have fewer friends because parents and grandparents supply that need in their life.) Middle children often engage in team sports or join a gang to find recognition and a sense of belonging. These children often leave home at an early age to avoid the frustration of being average.

Because middle children learn to negotiate and compromise at an early age, they often grow up to be well-adjusted adults. However, their penchant for peace may actually condition them toward codependency. Even though they may need professional help as an adult, they will seldom seek it when needed. Whereas firstborns demand help and lastborns expect to be cared for, middle children develop a spirit of independence and mental toughness that does not allow them to accept assistance except from their friends.

Middle children are great negotiators and learn at an early age how to make relationships work. This often influences them in the area of monogamy and commitment.

Even though being a middle child is a relatively safe position, it is often unfair. Therefore, middle children tend to view life through reality lenses rather than fantasy glasses. Unlike first- and lastborns, who often have a distorted view of life, middle children expect little from life and thus are seldom disappointed. Because firstborns have run interference for them, middle children often relate to a more relaxed parent. Balance is a key element in the lives of middle children.

It is important for parents of a middle child to refrain from the comparison trap. Comparing children is futile and pointless at best, while absolutely devastating and destructive at its worst. Middle children will probably develop good listening and negotiating skills because of their position in the family. If we help these middle children develop those skills, they will later thank us.

Negotiators and compromisers often make the best managers and leaders. When we assist our children to master these skills, we are helping them develop a valuable asset for the rest of their lives.

The Charmer (Lastborn)

A small lastborn child, assigned to the attic bedroom, was frightened during the night by a thunderstorm. After being assured by his mother that God would take care of him, he replied, "Well, you come up here and stay with God. I want to go down and sleep with Daddy."

It is difficult to argue with outgoing, charming, manipulative, affectionate lastborns. They are usually clowns or attention-getters, and according to the other siblings, spoiled rotten. The family curse on lastborns is to be viewed as both the smallest and the weakest forever. Often you will see a 5'6" firstborn introduce a 6'5" lastborn as "my little brother"! This often prompts lastborns to go through life constantly looking for praise and encouragement. Like Mark Twain, lastborns can often live a month off a good compliment.

Of all the sibling positions, lastborns are the most likely to be "people persons." Studies indicate that the babies of the family tend to gravitate toward people-oriented jobs.

Of all the sibling positions, lastborns are the most likely to be "people persons." Studies indicate that the babies of the family tend to gravitate toward people-oriented jobs. Leman tells about a used-car salesman who was so bubbly and friendly that without even trying he often sold the most cars each month. However, the manager (a firstborn) was constantly haranguing him about getting in his paperwork. Finally a psychologist told the manager to hire a secretary to do the paperwork for his top (lastborn) salesman and let him do what he did best, relate to people. A survey of the used-car lot revealed that all the salesmen were lastborns trying to work for a workaholic firstborn, who was making their life miserable by his constant demand for paperwork. Perhaps we parents need to develop the same understanding of our children in school, sports, and social activities.

The independent cockiness displayed by lastborns is often an attempt to cover up inner confusion. Impetuous and brash, lastborns rush in where angels fear to tread. They seldom consider consequences before they take action.

We who are parents of lastborns should help them accept responsibility and develop maturity. We should instill in them the habit of picking up after themselves. It is likely that by now, after having dealt with three or four children, we may find it easier to make the bed and pick up the room after lastborns rather than endure the hassle. Actually, we do them a great disservice when we perform these functions for them. We must help our lastborn children recognize the fine line between being the family clown and being obnoxious. This may be difficult, and it often requires discipline unwanted by either the child or the parent.

A little lastborn was smarting after being punished by his father for being obnoxious in front of houseguests. Shortly afterward the father tucked him into bed and knelt with him as he said his prayers. The prayer ended with all the usual blessings for all the family members except one.

It is important to remember that all children are unique, no matter what their birth order or temperament.

Then the mischievous lastborn turned to his father and announced, "I suppose you noticed that you weren't in it!"

We can learn to appreciate the timing and sense of humor of our lastborns. While it may be extremely difficult, we should avoid placing our lastborns in the spotlight more than we do our other children. We must refuse to cling to them as our last gasp of parenting. We can refuse to create in them an unhealthy dependence upon us. We must foster in them an independent spirit that is appropriate for honing their natural people skills.

It is important to remember that all children are unique, no matter what their birth order or temperament. The personality of our children is a combination of many factors: inherited temperament characteristics, birth order, culture, friends, and parental style—to name a few. Interestingly enough, it is often when studying our children's similarities that we discover their uniqueness.

Perhaps you can identify with a young mother's reaction to her child's abilities (or apparent lack of them) at a school track meet. The participants were in the final lap of a boys' one-mile run. The pack was bunched together except for two runners, who were leading by a few yards. As the runners rounded the last corner, the crowd was cheering wildly. In the midst of all this excitement it was easy to overlook a short, chubby kid who was running hopelessly last. He probably had difficulty walking a mile, much less running one. Nevertheless, there he was, pushing toward the finish line. His contorted red face revealed the supreme effort he was putting forth. It appeared that his entire body might actually explode at any moment.

Suddenly a frantic woman pressed through the noisy crowd, jumped up on the railing, and screamed, "Johnny, run faster! Run faster!" Her shrill voice carried above the din of the noisy crowd. Obviously she was the boy's mother.

A hopeless look spread across Johnny's face after he heard his mother shrieking at him. You could read the silent reply in his countenance: *Run faster? Run faster? If I could run any faster do you think I'd be dead last? Just what do you think is my problem, Mom? Do you think I forgot how to run? I'm running as fast as I can!*

As we attempt to understand our children, it is important that we show appreciation for the best effort our children put forth. It is not important for them to act like their brothers or sisters.

Thought Questions

1. What is your birth order, and how has it affected your personal relationships?

2. Reflect on how your birth order has influenced your parenting style.

3. How has birth order affected your children and their behavior?

CHAPTER 4

"Shut Up When I'm Talking to You!"

(Communicating With Your Child)

> *"A word aptly spoken is like apples of gold in settings of silver"* (Prov. 25:11, NIV).

The kindergarten teacher was instructing the children how to count and do simple arithmetic problems. "Johnny," the teacher asked, "can you tell me what is 1 and 1?"

"That's easy," said the little fellow, who had learned a lot by watching television. "It means one ball and one strike."

Three years later little Johnny was asked to write something with the word "adult" in it. The next day he turned in the following composition:

"Adults don't have any fun. Adults just sit around and talk. Adults don't do nothing. There is nothing duller than adultery."

Communication appears to be deceptively simple. Obviously it is not, since there are approximately 4,000 languages and dialects spoken in the world today! The English language has an 800,000-word vocabulary that is growing by more than a 1,000 words each year even though few people use more than 6,000 words in a lifetime. Journalists use only 20,000 words at the peak of their profession. The average farm laborer manages quite well with 1,600.

The English alphabet contains more than 29 quintillion (29,000,000,000,000,000,000) possible combinations. It has been estimated that if Shakespeare came back today, he would misunderstand almost half the words currently spoken. Language is sort of like the air we breathe. We take it for granted until it becomes polluted.

Communication is really not a simple task. Especially when we use the English language. Did you ever wonder why we *drive* on a *parkway* and *park* in a *driveway*? Since *pro* and *con* are opposites, does that mean that *congress* is the opposite of *progress*? How can a *fat* chance and a *slim* chance mean the same thing? How is it possible for your nose to *run* and your feet to *smell*?

If you assume that your children understand your instructions completely, remember the man who went to a local lumber yard and asked, "Do you have any 4 x 2s?"

The clerk responded, "You mean 2 x 4s, don't you?"

A puzzled look came over the man's face, and he said, "Just a moment, I'll check." He ran out to the car for a brief conversation and returned. "Yes, I mean 2 x 4s."

"How long do you want them?" inquired the clerk.

Again a puzzled look came over the man's face, and he ran back out to the car. Returning a few minutes later, he replied, "A long time, 'cause we're building a house."

Language is sort of like the air we breathe. We take it for granted until it becomes polluted.

According to students of the *Oxford English Dictionary*, the 500 most commonly used words in the English language have an average of 23 different meanings each. The word "round" is especially dense with meaning, with 70 distinctly different denotations.

English often doesn't follow predictable rules, yet parents appear certain that their children understand precisely what they mean.

A single, large ducklike bird is called a *goose* and two or more are *geese*, but *meese* is not the plural of *mouse*. Similarly, one small rodent is a *mouse* and many of them are *mice*, but the plural of *house* is not *hice*. If logic were to hold, then the plural of *pan* should be *pen* because the plural of *man* is *men*. One *foot* becomes two *feet*, but if you had more than one *boot*, you would not say that you had a pair of *beet*. And have you ever noticed that *tooth* is singular and *teeth* plural, yet the plural of *booth* is not *beeth*? If we say *he*, *his*, and *him*, wouldn't it be logical to say *she*, *shis*, and *shim*? (I am indebted to *7700 Illustrations*, item 2991.)

If we understand our children's temperament blends, we can communicate more effectively with them. Since we parents are assumed to have a greater degree of maturity than our children, it is suggested that we learn to adapt our communication style to accommodate our children's temperaments.

Sanguine—Sanguine children usually want to know people's opinions, especially their parents'. It is relatively easy for parents to communicate with sanguine children if it is done in an informal, flexible setting in which the children feel accepted. Unfriendly parents, who use negative body language and hostile voice intonations, will cause sanguine children to tune them out.

Dad asked Sanguine Sammy what he had learned at school. Enthusiastically Sammy described his geography lesson. Dad drummed his fingers impatiently while he waited for Sammy to finish. When Sammy paused for breath, Dad remarked cuttingly, "I bet you don't know where Afghanistan is."

Sammy admitted he didn't know, so Dad continued, "Well, for your information, it's next to Russia." Then in a contemptuous tone Dad added, "And you think you learned geography!"

If parents approach sanguine children with a critical, sarcastic, or demanding attitude, poor communication is likely to result. It is important for parents to focus on harmony, be friendly, and stay flexible. We parents should use humor whenever the situation gets really tense. Sanguine children will respond positively and understand the message much better in an informal, friendly, and supportive atmosphere.

Choleric—Choleric children are usually not interested in idle chitchat, even with Mom and Dad. They want to know who's in control. Once that is established, they want to know the bottom line in any communication. What do their parents expect? How far can the children go without getting into trouble? Where are the boundaries?

Little Choleric Cally was talking to her grandmother and inquired, "Grandma, how old are you?"

"Now, dear, you shouldn't ask people that question."

"How much do you weigh?" persisted Cally.

"Oh, honey, you shouldn't ask grown-ups how much they weigh. It isn't polite."

The next day Choleric Cally was back with a big smile on her face. "Grandma, I know how old you are. You're 62. And you weigh 140 pounds."

Astonished, Grandma inquired, "How do you know that?"

"You left your driver's license on the table, and I read it," replied the smiling Cally. "And I also found out something else, Grandma."

"What's that, child?"

"I saw on your driver's license that you got an F in sex."

Choleric children are strong-willed, competitive, and enterprising. They respond well to contests and rewards. If they are given authority to make decisions within specific boundaries, they will usually excel and may even "hear" what their parents have to say.

Increasing their responsibility, rather than restricting their freedom, is often the key to communicating successfully with choleric children. We can make them more accountable, while we give them the freedom to act. We can offer a challenge and stress the opportunities that are being made available to them.

Melancholy—Fairness is a key concept when communicating with melancholy children. They truly want to be helpful and do what is right. They also want their parents to be very specific and tell them exactly what is expected.

Melancholy Mindy came home from school with tears in her eyes.

"What's the matter?" asked her mother.

"I wish you'd let me take my bath in the morning before I go to school instead of at night before I go to bed."

"What difference does that make?" replied Mother.

"Every day at school," Mindy sobbed, "Miss Taylor tells everybody to stand up who had a bath today. And I haven't been able to stand up one time since school started three months ago!"

Because of their obedience, melancholy children expect that their parents will treat them fairly. Respect is important when speaking to a melancholy. It must be seen in the parents' body language and heard in their tone of voice. Melancholies need parents to understand their idealistic nature.

Melancholy children respond poorly to criticism or ridicule. It is best for parents to work together when attempting behavior changes in their melancholy children. Melancholies naturally strive toward excellence, and they love to please their parents. Parents need to frequently praise melancholy children to keep communication channels open.

Phlegmatic—Phlegmatic children desire full knowledge of work assignments for the entire family. They want to be assured that all are doing their share. Phlegmatic children usually carry out specific instructions, but we should not expect them to be self-starters. Changes confuse and discourage them. Phlegmatics respond best to behavior change requests when they are linked with something they have already learned.

Phlegmatic Pam was only 3 years old, but Mother was trying to teach her to use proper English. She repeatedly explained to Pam, "Never say, 'I don't have *none*.' Always say, 'I don't have *any*.' "

Mother had been working with Pam on this rule for several weeks when one morning, on their way to church, the family met two Catholic nuns walking toward them. Pam shouted, "Oh, Daddy, look at the anys."

The two sisters stopped and looked at Pam. Embarrassed, Mother quickly tried to correct Pam. "Honey, they are not anys, they are *nuns*."

Obviously dismayed, Pam replied, "Well, Mommy, make up your mind!"

What phlegmatic children have learned in early childhood is not easily unlearned later. It may be difficult to explain to phlegmatic children that what was appropriate behavior last year is no longer acceptable now that they are more mature. Phlegmatics change slowly—if at all. They also do not respond well to highly emotional outbursts and unexpected changes in rules.

In addition to understanding children's temperament blends, it is beneficial for parents to determine the communication input preference of their children. There are three main inputs through which we communicate: hearing (auditory), seeing (visual), and feelings (kinesthetic).

In addition to understanding children's temperament blends, it is beneficial for parents to determine the communication input preference of their children. There are three main inputs through which we communicate: hearing (auditory), seeing (visual), and feelings (kinesthetic). While it is possible for everyone to communicate through all three inputs, most of us have a preferred input. This primary mode is combined with a secondary backup that may be used for additional information or when a person is under stress.

Auditory—Children who depend on the spoken word for communication are primarily auditory. They often take literally what is said, even if it is a figure of speech. Frequently they are unable to read body language or sense underlying feelings. Choleric children are often auditory.

A mother consulted her pastor because her oldest son was using too much profanity. Being from the "spare the rod and spoil the child" school of theology, the pastor advised her to slap him every time he uttered a profanity.

As her two sons came to the breakfast table the next morning, the mother asked, "What would you like for breakfast?"

"I want some of those _____ Post Toasties!" exclaimed the oldest son. The mother reared back and slapped him so hard that he fell off his chair and landed with a thud on the floor.

Responses such as "I *hear* you loud and clear" or "It *sounds* good to me" indicate the child is receiving through auditory input.

As he sat dazed, she turned to the other son and asked, "Now, what do you want for breakfast?"

Stammering meekly, the other son replied, "Well, one thing's for certain, I don't want any Post Toasties!"

Parents should make certain their message is properly understood when they are speaking to an auditory child. Responses such as "I *hear* you loud and clear" or "It *sounds* good to me" indicate the child is receiving through auditory input.

Visual—Visual children use mental images when talking, remembering, or thinking. Parents will often observe visual children glancing to their upper right or upper left when thinking. This indicates that they are visually sorting through their memory bank. Words used by auditory parents can be misunderstood by visual children. Word pictures are more important to visuals than are precise definitions. Sanguines are often visual.

Seven-year-old Sally stood in front of her parents at a supermarket when a midget-sized adult crossed nearby. She overheard her mother tell her father in a stage whisper, "It's the genes that make the difference."

A few days later, in school, a little boy asked the teacher why some people do not grow as tall as everyone else. Before the teacher could respond, Sally waved her hand frantically and jumped to her feet. "It's because they wear tight blue pants!" she exclaimed triumphantly.

Sometimes visual children read more into a visual message than was intended by the sender. A teenage girl was browsing through the library when she came across a book titled *How to Reach Men, How to Hold Men, How to Win Men, and How It Has Been Done!* Quickly she checked out the book and rushed home with her prize. She was greatly disappointed as she later read the fine print at the bottom of the page: "A Manual of Useful Information on How to Build a Men's Bible Class."

> **To determine if a child is visual, listen for phrases such as "I *see* what you're saying," "That *looks* good to me," or "How does that *appear* to you?"**

To determine if a child is visual, listen for phrases such as "I *see* what you're saying," "That *looks* good to me," or "How does that *appear* to you?"

Kinesthetic—Kinesthetic children relate to life's experiences through their feelings. It isn't so much what their parents say as how they say it. The tone of voice is more important than the actual words. Body language speaks so loudly it is sometimes difficult to communicate with a kinesthetic unless parents are tuned in to the child's feelings. Melancholy children are often primarily kinesthetic.

Lucy is talking to Charlie Brown about the inability to understand love. "You know what I don't understand? I don't understand love!" exclaims Lucy.

"You can't explain love," replies Charlie Brown. "I can recommend a book or a poem or a painting, but I can't explain love."

"Well, try, Charlie Brown. Try!"

"Well, OK. Let's say I see this beautiful, cute little girl walk by . . ."

"Why does she have to be cute? Huh? Why can't someone fall in love with someone with freckles and a big nose? Explain that!" shouts Lucy.

"Well, maybe you're right. Let's just say I see this girl with a great big nose walk by . . ."

"I didn't say *great* big nose!" insisted Lucy.

With a deep sigh Charlie concludes, "You not only can't explain love—you can't even talk about it!"

Parents may feel the same way in discussions with a kinesthetic child. Feelings overshadow words and provide definitions that may be quite different from those found in a dictionary.

Often kinesthetic children find it almost impossible to respond to an auditory parent. What the auditory parent *hears* is not what the child *feels*. What the kinesthetic child *hears* is not what the auditory parent said. Neither can understand the other. Finally the child may be reduced to sobbing in frustration, "You never *understand* anything!"

What help is available to avoid these common pitfalls in communication? By becoming familiar with the following styles and techniques, parents can increase their ability to communicate. However, the key is more than knowledge; it is practice . . . practice . . . practice!

Key phrases that may identify a kinesthetic child are "I have a bad *feeling* about this" or "I sense something is wrong today."

The Echo—One of the easiest techniques to clarify communication is to behave like an echo. Before you add anything new to the conversation, you first repeat what the other person has just said. While this technique should not be used ad nauseum, a parent's inability to hear a child's feelings will become clear with the first echo. The key to being a proper echo is to pause after restating the child's message so corrections can be made before continuing.

Child: "Why do I have to keep practicing on this dumb piano?" (initial message)

Parent: "You seem upset because I have asked you to practice your piano. Do you want to play with your friends instead?" (summary of thoughts and feelings as perceived by parent)

Child: "Yes, I want to play ball with them." (acknowledgment that summary was correct)

Parent: "I'm sorry practicing the piano upsets you. Let me explain why I feel it's important for you to learn to play the piano and why I want you to practice now . . ." (introduces new material)

It is important for parents also to teach their children to echo (summarize) what the parent has just said before the children can introduce a new thought of their own. Admittedly this slows down the communication process, but it also teaches both parties to listen carefully and summarize accurately before responding. Too often parents and children spend a great deal of time arguing and very little time communicating.

The Informer—Too often parents and children fail to complete their thoughts. They assume the other person can somehow read their mind. The following true story illustrates the necessity of providing complete information.

In a small town the volunteer fire department's telephone was answered by the police officer on duty, who in turn would sound the fire whistle to rally the volunteers to action. One morning the chief of police had just come on duty when the fire department phone rang. "Hello, fire department," answered the chief.

A female voice shouted frantically, "Send the fire truck!" and immediately slammed down the receiver.

Stunned, the police chief sat motionless, not knowing what to do. In a few minutes the phone rang again. Quickly he answered, "Fire department." Again the hysterical voice screamed, "Send the fire truck!" and hung up.

Realizing that someone's house was on fire but not knowing the address, the chief rushed outside to scan the sky for smoke. While outside, he devised a plan to keep the caller from hanging up so quickly if she phoned again. Soon the phone rang, and the chief answered by asking, "Where's the fire?"

Still hysterical, the woman screamed, "In the kitchen!" and slammed down the receiver!

To be a true *informer* you must provide enough information for the other party to respond adequately. It is not helpful to tell children, "Shut up when I'm talking to you!" It is important to keep them talking. Even in their anger or disappointment you will receive valuable information about their state of being.

The Snafu—When a message comes through so garbled that the other party acts irresponsibly, we say that a snafu has occurred. My mother gave me a plaque that reads: "I know that you believe you understand what I said. But I am not sure you realize that what you heard is not what I meant."

This is often the case in communication. When a message comes through with a garbled meaning, ask for clarification.

I read somewhere about a census taker who knocked on the door of a mountaineer's shack. The old-timer came to the door and asked what the guest wanted.

Knowing that some mountain people distrust strangers, the census taker explained, "The president has sent me across the country to find out how many people live in the United States."

The mountaineer replied, "Son, I'm sorry you came all the way out here to ask me, 'cause I ain't got the foggiest idea."

Unfortunately, it is relatively easy to encounter snafus in communication. Words used may not match body language. Eyes may say yes while the words say no. Feelings and past experiences may create a misunderstanding.

Snafus often develop when a message has two or more possible meanings. Considering that 500 of the most commonly used words have more than 20 different meanings each, it is easy to understand how a snafu can take place.

A pastor was proud of his new loose-leaf Bible and decided to use it when he preached a series from Genesis. In his second sermon of the series he preached about the Fall. He began reading, "And Adam said to Eve . . ." At this point he had to turn the page to complete the verse. But after flipping the page, he paused, looked puzzled for a few seconds, and finally realized what had happened. With an embarrassed look he mumbled, "It looks like a leaf is missing."

Clear communication does not necessarily result in total agreement. Parents who expect clarity of communication to mean consensus of opinion may be in for a rude awakening. Communication should reveal the issues and be clearly understood, but it does not guarantee agreement.

A father received a letter from his son at college. The young man wanted money. In reply the father made a certain clarification: "I'm enclosing the $10 as you requested in your letter. Incidentally, son, $10 is written with one zero rather than two."

Body Language—Perhaps one of the most important aspects of family communication is body language. If parents want to prevent giving mixed signals to their children and causing a snafu, they need to practice and teach body language that is appropriate for the intended message. The most important communication tool is not the tongue but the eyes. What we do with our eyes is far more important than what we say with our tongue. Our words may sound sweet, but if our eyes flash fire, children will get a message of insincerity and dishonesty. If we break eye contact too soon, we may appear weak. If we hold eye contact too long, it may be perceived as a challenge or threat.

Clear communication does not necessarily result in total agreement. Parents who expect clarity of communication to mean consensus of opinion may be in for a rude awakening. Communication should reveal the issues and be clearly understood, but it does not guarantee agreement.

Parents should also learn proper gestures that will provide clues to the message being sent. The basic nod indicates agreement. The wrinkled brow says "Your message is unclear; please repeat or restate." The upward glance says "You're boring me" or "I'm searching for the proper words."

Touch is a tremendous communicator and can offer instant affirmation, encouragement, or comfort. Parents will find it extremely beneficial to cuddle their children while talking to them. Even teens appreciate a sincere hug or pat on the back, especially if it isn't done in front of their peers.

We can learn to lean forward when we talk to our children. This will assure them that we are interested in what they are saying. We should not allow ourselves to become distracted during a conversation. We will not have to lean forward long in talking with our children because they have a very short attention span, especially when it involves their parents.

The Encourager—We parents cannot offer too much approval to our children, unless we fail to offer proper correction. Paul noted the necessity of encouragement when he wrote to the church members at Thessalonica: "Therefore encourage one another and build each other up, just as in fact you are doing" (1 Thess. 5:11, NIV).

Someone once said, "If you can't say something nice, it is better to say nothing at all." We can practice telling our children, "Thanks for listening so carefully. It means a lot to me. I appreciate you! I love you! You are a gift from God!"

"Everyone enjoys giving good advice, and how wonderful it is to be able to say the right thing at the right time!" (Prov. 15:23, TLB).

The Peacemaker—It is possible for parents to win the battle with their children and still lose the war. If we win an argument with the child but create hostility, what have we gained? Only an enemy. One of the purposes of communication is to clarify feelings, misunderstandings, word definitions, and whatever else is not clearly understood. As parents we need to spend less time

"Everyone enjoys giving good advice, and how wonderful it is to be able to say the right thing at the right time!"

manipulating and more time communicating. That doesn't necessarily mean more talking; it may indicate a need to listen more. "Don't talk so much. You keep putting your foot in your mouth. Be sensible and turn off the flow!" (Prov. 10:19, TLB).

If we want to be effective peacemakers, we must learn to tolerate negative emotions in our children and allow our children to express negative feelings at the appropriate time. Although we will not tolerate our children to vent their negative emotions at the supermarket, we should allow them to express such feelings as soon as it is appropriate. We can learn to listen carefully to what our children are saying. Temper tantrums are not on the acceptable list (see chapter on discipline), but allowing children to unload their negative feelings is important for parents and children.

Parents may find it helpful to claim this Bible promise and teach it to their children: "It is better to be slow-tempered than famous; it is better to have self-control than to control an army" (Prov. 16:32, TLB).

It is important for us parents to acknowledge our children's misbehavior without accepting blame and guilt. It is correct to say, "I'm sorry that you hurt and are angry." (This expresses empathy without attributing cause or blame.) Assuming you have not personally injured the child, it is not correct to say, "I'm sorry I hurt you." (This implies accepting the blame and guilt for their negative behavior.) Children must be taught at an early age that they alone are responsible for their feelings and behavior. Teaching them to control their behavior, to accept their feelings, and to talk through their problems is an important part of their education.

"The goal of communication is not happiness; it's giving and receiving honest messages about each other. This process may or may not carry with it feelings of happiness. . . . Communication is hard enough without happiness murking up the water. Happiness may be a by-product of communication, but it shouldn't be the goal of communication" (Thomas Smith, *Marriage and Family Living*, p. 11).

Perhaps the bottom line for family communication is *sensitivity* and *tact*. It may be more important to understand what children are feeling than what they are saying.

Perhaps the bottom line for family communication is *sensitivity* and *tact*. It may be more important to understand what children are feeling than what they are saying. Communication is the single most important factor in good parent-child relationships. And we need to remember that we are always communicating even when we may not be speaking words.

According to some statisticians, the average parent spends at least one fifth of his or her life talking. In a single day each parent uses enough words to fill a 54-page book. In one year's time a parent will fill 132 400-page books. On a normal day we parents will use between 25,000 and 30,000 words. Is it any wonder we are often misunderstood—and sometimes misunderstand others?

Thought Questions

1. Recall an incident in which there was definite miscommunication between you and one of your children.

2. Reflect on how you communicate. Do you find it difficult to move in and out of your favorite style? Why or why not?

3. Recall a personal incident in which body language and spoken words were not compatible. How did you feel?

CHAPTER 5

"Can't You Ever Do Anything Right?"

(Controlling Parental Anger)

> *"And now a word to you parents. Don't keep on scolding and nagging your children, making them angry and resentful. Rather, bring them up with the loving discipline the Lord himself approves, with suggestions and godly advice" (Eph. 6:4, TLB).*

As he turns his car into the driveway, Tom feels the flush of anger rising up inside him. There lying across the entire width of the driveway are three bicycles. "That's it!" he fumes to himself. "If I've told those kids once, I've told them a hundred times, 'Put your bikes away when you get home.' Why can't they listen? I've even asked Cindy to remind the kids when they come home from school. No one ever listens around here. No one puts away bikes or anything else. Maybe I should just throw them in the trash! That would fix them!" Tom furiously lays on the car horn.

Prepared for an emergency, Cindy runs frantically out of the house. As soon as she comes into view, Tom starts yelling at the top of his voice and gesturing wildly at the bikes. Cindy pauses, casts a withering glance in his direction, and stomps back into the house.

Tom slams the shift lever into park and stalks toward the offending bicycles. With the strength of uncontrolled anger, he throws each bike into the yard and marches back to his car. Yanking the shift lever into low, he leaves a black mark on the driveway (that he will spend most of Sunday morning trying to remove) and lurches into the garage.

Storming into the kitchen, Tom slams the door behind him and yells for the kids. "The kids are across the street at a birthday party, and don't you dare spoil this day for them!" Cindy warns.

"What are they doing across the street when their bikes are not put away?" Tom demands.

"They were late getting home from school, and I didn't think to check," Cindy responds defensively. "Why are you always getting on the kids about their bikes, anyway? Maybe if you'd put your dirty socks in the hamper instead of on the bathroom floor, the kids might learn to put their bikes away," she screams.

"Speaking of leaving things out," Tom interrupts, "why is the bread still sitting here on the counter from this morning? Maybe the reason the kids haven't learned to take care of their bikes is because you leave the kitchen looking like a disaster zone. I'm tired of this place looking like a mess every day."

Does this sound familiar? What has happened? How did Tom and Cindy get out of control so quickly? What is the real source of their anger? How can we go from a respectable Dr. Jekyll to a hateful Mr. Hyde in 30 seconds? The spirit of Edward Hyde, Dr. Jekyll's evil side, seems to live in most of us to one degree or another. The correct word for this side of our character was identified by the apostle Paul: "So then it is no longer I that do it, but *sin* which dwells within me" (Rom. 7:17, RSV).

A pet peeve is a simple, nonlethal, nontoxic, relatively mundane behavior of human nature that just churns our insides and grates our nerves until we explode.

I am sure you realize that most of us have anger buttons just waiting to be pushed by some unsuspecting person. One of the more easily reached buttons is a pet peeve. This button is easy to push because it seems so insignificant to others. When someone pushes our pet peeve button, we often overreact. This button often becomes even more sensitive when we have difficulty explaining to others (and ourselves) why it makes us so angry.

A pet peeve is a simple, nonlethal, nontoxic, relatively mundane behavior of human nature that just churns our insides and grates our nerves until we explode. Tom's pet peeves were bicycles in the driveway and bread on the kitchen counter. Cindy's pet peeve was dirty socks on the bathroom floor, within smelling distance of the hamper!

One problem with pet peeves in a family is that children often become caught in the cross fire—at least until they get old enough to establish some pet peeves of their own. Then they too become part of the anger problem and pass it on to the next generation.

Families often develop comfortable problems as an outlet for pet peeves and other hidden anger. Tom and Cindy will not mention bicycles, bread, or socks for many weeks, because these comfortable problems serve as an emotional garbage can. All the peeves and pressure that have built up since the last explosion have been dumped into them with impunity, and neither Tom nor Cindy will mention them again . . . until the next explosion. However, this problem isolates Tom and Cindy from any meaningful conversation that might solve the real problems. It has become a game at which both are knowledgeable players.

Another anger button is reactionary anger. A customer service representative at a major department store recalls one customer who became so angry over his bill that he exclaimed, "You make me so think I can't mad straight!"

Have you ever said something in the heat of anger and later wondered why you said it? Actually, it has to do with the way your brain is designed.

One section of your brain controls motor skills, which provide coordination and dexterity for all the muscle activity of your body.

Another section allows the storage of thoughts and information—we call it the memory. Memory, of course, helps you keep your life in order and remember the names of your spouse and children.

A third section of your brain deals with the intellect and allows you to reason. This section makes you a rational human being (most of the time) and helps you determine cause and effect.

A fourth section controls your emotions. It is this section of the brain that we will be talking about in this chapter. Once a thought activates this section, it becomes strong enough to override all the other sections of the brain. Under its influence we will perform feats of strength not normally possible, do things we normally would not do, and say things that we later regret.

An elderly lady drove into a shopping mall parking lot in her brand-new, expensive, and large Lincoln Town Car. The lot was crowded, but she eventually found a parking place that required parallel parking. Pulling past the space, she was preparing to back in when a young man driving a little sports car zoomed into her parking place.

"Why did you do that?" the woman shouted angrily as she jumped from her car.

"Because I'm young and because I'm quick!" the young man replied sarcastically. With that he walked off toward a nearby store. Returning a few minutes later, he found the elderly woman using her new car as a battering ram, with his little sports car the recipient.

"Why are you doing that?" he yelled as she backed up to hit his car one more time.

"Because I'm old and because I'm rich," the elderly woman screamed above the din of smoking tires and crunching metal.

When the emotion section of the brain takes over, we find ourselves saying and doing things outside our normal behavior pattern. That's because everything is now filtered through our anger, and we cannot reason or act rationally when emotion is in control. Unfortunately, that is often the exact moment we choose to discipline a child or respond to our spouse.

Child abuse victims are more prone to a wide range of ills, from drug use to marital problems. The sad fact is that one in every six Americans was seriously abused as a child.

I remember reading about a man who was bitten by a dog, so he had the dog impounded for examination. When he went to the doctor to find out the results, the physician replied, "I'm terribly sorry, but the tests are positive. The dog has rabies, and you may contract the disease."

With that, the man took out a pad and pencil and began to write furiously.

"Now, now," assured the doctor, "you don't have to write your will. I'll pull you through."

"Will nothing," snapped the man. "This is a list of people I'm going to bite!"

Some parents are like a rabid dog looking for someone to bite. Such parents are often guilty of child abuse, which is triggered by their anger buttons. Tragically, the effects of the abuse continue long after the physical or emotional trauma has ceased. Young women who were sexually abused as children are much more likely to suffer date rape as adults. Child abuse victims are also more prone to a wide range of ills, from drug use to marital problems. The sad fact is that one in every six Americans was seriously abused as a child.

Repressed anger is another button that may cause us to switch to the emotional section of our brain. Some chronically angry or depressed parents are actually suffering from repressed anger. They are aware that they have a little problem with anger, but they try to keep it in check. Occasionally they are unsuccessful in holding back the anger, and they explode. One of their greatest fears is that they will lose control, so they dwell on being in control much of the time. It is this fear that often allows inner anger to build up inside until someone touches the now sensitive trigger, and the result is abuse or divorce. The choleric temperament is especially vulnerable to chronic anger, but it is the melancholy and phlegmatic who repress it the most.

I counseled with a man who had so much inner anger that he was almost impossible to live with or work with. He was so caustic on his factory job that even though he was not a supervisor, they provided him with a private room so he could work alone. Because of his seniority they could not fire him, so they kept him out of everyone else's way. His home life was a complete disaster. Both he and his wife had been previously married. She had children from her previous marriage, and they could not stand their new stepfather. The couple also had a baby of their own, and the wife feared for its safety when the father was in one of his rages. She also feared for her other children and herself.

Counseling seemed to have little effect upon his anger. He admitted that he had a little problem with anger, but he could not grasp the magnitude of his situation. Eventually his new wife divorced him and received full custody of his only child, and he was alone with his anger once again.

He still finds it almost impossible to control his anger even though he is a Christian.

Depression may be another symptom of repressed anger. Depressed individuals are often unaware that they have an anger problem. Usually they are fearful of rejection or being disliked. Thus they try to please everyone even while they themselves are seething in their subconscious. Sometimes they will admit to being a little annoyed but seldom to being really angry. They are often confused about their feelings and describe themselves as doing a "slow burn" at times. Because they have few uncontrolled outbursts, other individuals think these depressed people have a handle on their anger. Unfortunately, the handle points inward, and every time these depressed people pull it they dump more anger inside themselves. People with a melancholy temperament are the most likely to become victims of their own anger.

A melancholy salesman driving along on a dark, lonely country road one rainy night suddenly felt the *thump-thump* of a flat tire. When he opened the trunk, he discovered that the lug wrench was missing. Frustrated, he looked down the road and saw the yard light of a farmhouse. Pulling his jacket over his head, he set out through the driving rain to borrow a lug wrench. *Surely the farmer will have a lug wrench,* he thought.

As he got closer to the house, he mused, *Of course, it is late at night, and he might be asleep. Maybe he won't even answer the door. Even if he does, he'll probably be angry because I've awakened him.*

An old Chinese proverb says, "Holding on to anger is like grasping a hot coal with the intention of throwing it at someone else. You are the one who gets burned."

Stumbling through the dark and soaked to the skin as water sloshed in his shoes, he reached the sidewalk leading to the farmhouse door. *Even if the farmer does answer the door, he'll probably yell at me for waking him up at this hour.* This thought made the salesman angry. *What right does this farmer have to refuse to lend me a lug wrench? After all, here I am stranded in the middle of nowhere, soaked to the skin, and this selfish clod refuses to lend me a stupid lug wrench!*

A few more steps and the salesman was at the front door. He banged on the door loudly. A light went on upstairs, the window opened, and a voice called out, "Who is it?"

White with rage, the salesman yelled back, "You know very well who it is! And you can just keep your blasted lug wrench. I wouldn't borrow it now if it was the last one on earth!"

Sometimes melancholy parents find themselves visualizing a worst-case scenario when a carefree (which they define as irresponsible) sanguine child is late returning from a date. When it becomes apparent that the child will not be home on time, melancholy parents begin to worry about an auto accident, kidnapping, abduction, etc. Repeatedly running these scenes through the mind puts their brain into "instant replay," and it reruns all the negative and irresponsible things the child has ever done. The parents' anger usually reaches the boiling point just as the unsuspecting child returns with a perfectly logical and truthful explanation. Unfortunately, melancholy parents explode into an uncontrolled tirade.

Those who repress their anger can also find it difficult to forgive their children or feel forgiven themselves. If we want to let go of anger, we must first acknowledge that it exists. Yet fear may prevent us from dealing with such inner feelings, so they linger on and make us even more sensitive to every new hurt. An old Chinese proverb says, "Holding on to anger is like grasping a hot coal with the intention of throwing it at someone else. You are the one who gets burned."

William Blake wrote about repressed anger in his poem, "A Poison Tree."

> I was angry with my friend:
> I told my wrath, my wrath did end.
> I was angry with my foe
> I told it not, my wrath did grow.
> And I watered it in fears,
> Night and morning with my tears;
> And I sunned it with smiles,
> And with soft deceitful wiles.
> And it grew both day and night,
> Till it bore an apple bright.
> And my foe beheld it shine,
> And he knew that it was mine,
> And into my garden stole,
> When the night had veiled the pole;
> In the morning glad I see
> My foe outstretched beneath the tree.

Repressed anger can actually be transferred from one generation to the next without the conscious knowledge of either the parent or child.

Melvin and Sue were in their late 50s and their son, Jack, who was 30 something, still lived with them. Jack had been married, but was now divorced and without a job. Each time he tried to strike out on his own some crisis occurred, and he ended up back home again. It seemed that his parents were always there to bail him out.

Both parents were angry with Jack. Actually, Melvin was furious! He thought that his son was lazy, refused to pay any rent, used foul language in his mother's presence, and was more of a bum than a son. Whenever Melvin would express his anger at Jack, the response was always the same: "Throw me out if you don't like it! I dare you!"

Melvin was also angry with Sue. He felt that she protected Jack too much. Whenever Melvin tried to get him out of the house, Sue would refuse to back him up. Melvin complained, "Sometimes I think you care more about his feelings than mine. Ever since we've been married, my feelings have never been important to you. You always want things done your way, and I just have to go along with it to keep the peace." Melvin also insinuated that Sue's protectiveness actually caused Jack to be lazy and irresponsible.

Repressed anger can actually be transferred from one generation to the next without the conscious knowledge of either the parent or child.

Jack became defensive, of course, and announced that he was leaving for good. This upset Sue. She stopped fighting with Melvin, as if to tell Jack there would be no more fighting if he would just stay. Melvin, realizing he was outnumbered, said nothing. Jack stayed. But each member of the family was seething in anger.

During family counseling Melvin was asked, "How did you get along with your mother when she was alive?"

Melvin curtly replied, "I didn't! I even took care of her after Dad died, but all she did was criticize everything I did."

Sue confirmed Melvin's analysis. "Yes, Melvin did make a lot of sacrifices to care for his mother, but she never gave him any credit."

Melvin interrupted, "Much of my life I've felt spineless. And it's hard not to view Jack in the same light when he acts so irresponsibly and seems afraid to stick with a job."

For the first time Melvin realized that his anger toward his son was fueled by his repressed anger toward his mother and himself. "I've been irresponsible all these years. Every time I sat back and let my wife or mother make my decisions for me, I was acting irresponsibly. That wasn't fair to any of us."

Whenever anger is so deep and longstanding, it is usually because there is something about yourself that makes you angry too. Recognizing that anger and confronting it is the first step toward freedom from repressed anger.

Melvin found that he was angry at Jack . . . angry at Sue . . . angry at his mother . . . and angry at himself. Jack found that he was angry at his dad . . . angry at his mom . . . angry at his ex-wife . . . and angry at himself. If he had been a father, he probably would have passed on his repressed anger to his child as well.

Whenever anger is so deep and longstanding, it is usually because there is something about yourself that makes you angry too. Recognizing that anger and confronting it is the first step toward freedom from repressed anger.

Manipulative anger is another familiar anger button. Children learn to use this anger button at an early age because it gets instant results. If a child wants something, all he or she needs to do is throw a tantrum, and the intimidated parent will give in. Choleric children develop this skill at a very early age.

At breakfast one morning, 8-year-old choleric Cutie Pie pushed her corn flakes away and protested loudly, "I will *not* eat this stuff! I won't eat *any* breakfast unless there's somethin' gooder!"

Mother inquired, "Well, what would you like?"

"I want a big, fat, juicy worm," sniffed the little girl.

Father was dispatched to the garden and returned with a worm, which he presented to Cutie Pie.

"I want it cooked," she screamed.

Mother rolled the worm in butter, breaded it, and dropped it into the frying pan until it turned a golden brown.

When she handed it to her spoiled daughter, she was greeted with more tears. "I want *Daddy* to eat half of it!" she pouted.

Reluctantly Daddy closed his eyes and gulped down half the worm. This prompted another session of loud wailing and whining.

"What's the matter *now*?" Mother inquired in exasperation. "Didn't Daddy eat half the worm like you wanted?"

"Yes," wailed Cutie Pie, "but he ate the half *I* wanted!"

Studies show that during preschool years boys tend to have more temper tantrums than girls. Perhaps it is better tolerated in boys. But the girls seem to catch up rapidly once school begins. It seems that some never outgrow the manipulative anger of temper tantrums. I read about a man who divorced his wife because she took his false teeth and held them for a $2 ransom!

Adults also tend to use manipulative anger (temper tantrums) when it comes to disciplining children. Because most kids tend to obey when they are being screamed at by an adult, children's obedience serves as a reinforcement to the parents' tantrums. However, children are quick to discover that they need not obey until their parents lose their temper. It should be noted that adults who throw temper tantrums are not respected by other adults any more than they are by their own children.

While driving down a back road in Idaho one afternoon, I came to an area where a work crew was trimming trees. Just before the work area was a woman with a caution flag. Her duty was to slow traffic. There was not another car on the road, and I was able to pull into the other lane, slow to a safe speed, and continue past the crew trimming trees. Evidently I was not slowing to whatever speed she had in mind, because she began to yell obscenities at me as I passed.

Amused, I looked in my rearview mirror just in time to see her throw her flag down on the road and jump up and down on it. Such behavior did not bolster my confidence in her ability to slow traffic!

Sometimes parental attempts at child discipline degenerate into temper tantrums, and both the parents and the children are embarrassed. My wife recalls arriving home from a double date a few minutes past her curfew. She lingered in the car, saying goodbye, longer than she probably should have, but she was shocked to hear the house door open and see her father come out to the car. He was clothed only in his undershirt and jockey shorts. Needless to say, she paid more careful attention to the curfew after that incident!

I do not want you to think that anger is a bad emotion. There are a number of myths that have been taught as fact among many Christians. The following is a partial list, but will provide some food for thought:

1. It's not OK to feel angry.
2. Anger is a waste of time and energy.
3. Real Christians never feel angry.
4. We shouldn't feel angry, even when we do.
5. We'll lose all control if we get angry.
6. Other people should never feel angry toward us.
7. If other people are angry at us, we made them feel that way, and it is our responsibility to "fix" their feelings.

Everyone should be quick to listen, slow to speak and slow to become angry, for man's anger does not bring about the righteous life that God desires" (James 1:19, 20, NIV).

8. If we feel angry, someone else made us feel that way and it is that person's responsibility to "fix" our feelings.

9. If we are angry at someone, the relationship is over, and that person must exit our life.

10. If someone feels angry at us, it means that person doesn't love us anymore.

11. Anger is a sinful emotion.
12. It's OK to feel angry only when we can justify our feelings.

Anger is an emotion given by God and instilled in each one of us at conception. Admitting that the emotion of anger is from God is the first step. Scripture tells us that we are all sinners. When we have a problem with anger, it is usually when the sinful side of our nature is in control. It is this sinful, destructive side of anger that we need to confront and control. God has provided, for our protection, a simple formula that works every time.

"My dear brothers, take note of this: Everyone should be quick to listen, slow to speak and slow to become angry, for man's anger does not bring about the righteous life that God desires" (James 1:19, 20, NIV).

Control 1: *Be quick to listen.*

In order to really listen, we must use both our eyes and ears. The optic and auditory nerves send messages to the cortex (the processing center) for interpretation. Based upon its previous programming, the cortex sends its interpretation of these messages to the limbic system. If the cortex tells the limbic system that we dislike what we have seen or heard, the limbic system responds by triggering the emotion of anger, which is accompanied by a sympathetic release of body chemicals. These chemicals, in turn, affect the ability of the cortex to control our thinking, speaking, and motor functions.

Unfortunately, sometimes the cortex interprets the messages in a negative manner when no offense was intended. Because of previous conditioning, the cortex may respond with the mad message through implication or association. If we are depressed, the cortex may misinterpret the messages from our eyes and ears and send a false alert to our limbic system. If we are under stress, our limbic system is already in control of our cortex, and we may find it difficult to maintain control of our thinking patterns.

Much to my shame, I recall a painful incident with my son when anger had complete control of my cortex. We were visiting another family, and I did not feel Mitch was behaving properly, so I excused the two of us and we went to a private bedroom to talk. Perhaps I should rephrase that statement. We went to a private bedroom where I would talk and he would listen. I had no intention of listening. I was embarrassed because we were visiting my senior pastor, and I wondered what he must think of all this.

As I confronted Mitch, he tried to answer my questions, but this only heated my anger to the boiling point. I lost control and hit him on the ear with my cupped hand. The impact of the compressed air in his ear from my cupped hand was extremely painful for him, and I felt intense shame, guilt, and remorse. Holding him close to me while he cried, I prayed to God that my anger would not cause him any hearing disability (thank God it didn't).

This incident is permanently recorded on my "instant replay" and will always be there to remind me of the danger of uncontrolled anger and the necessity of being quick to listen.

God recognizes that sin often interrupts the perfect process He originally built into the human body to deal with emotion. Therefore, He has provided us with an antidote for sin, His Son. If we let Christ control our cortex, we will be less liable to be angry, since He will already be meeting our basic needs. That does not mean, however, that we will never become angry. Anger is a normal emotion. It does mean that He will not allow our anger to be uncontrolled. It also means that our anger will be triggered less frequently by our own selfish desires and more often by a truly righteous cause as exemplified by Christ. Most anger in us sinful humans is caused by our self-pity rather than righteous indignation. Therefore, when Christ is in control of our life, sinful anger (that which is selfish in nature) will be eliminated.

With Jesus' thoughts loaded into our computer (cortex), we will have access to His thoughts when our cortex interprets the messages it receives. Therefore, it is important to listen to God as well as our body messages. By talking to God, we will find a willing Listener who will help us sort through our feelings about ourselves and others.

Control 2: *Be slow to speak.*

Most anger in us sinful humans is caused by our self-pity rather than righteous indignation. Therefore, when Christ is in control of our life, sinful anger (that which is selfish in nature) will be eliminated.

One of the best ways to control hasty speech is to pray before speaking. This is especially important when we are disciplining a child. We can ask God to take control of our anger as soon as we feel the first flush from our limbic system. The protection of prayer is only a thought away and will help us see the Lord's perspective before we act. When we are tempted to react in anger to a child, we must *stop*! If we find ourselves unable to pray at that moment, we can try one of the following.

We can lower our voice when talking to the child, actually whispering our message while we maintain eye contact. Often this will get the child's undivided attention and provide the teachable moment. If we find our anger increasing at that moment, then we should break eye contact so that we will not feel challenged. Often the fuel for uncontrolled anger is found in the eyes. If we feel anger continuing to build, we can intentionally look another way and in a calm tone make our request or share our feelings. By refusing to make eye contact until we are in control again, we can stop the wrong behavior.

Controlling our response is especially important when we feel the flush of anger. If we can control our emotions before they get out of hand, we will not have to rebuild the relationship with our child. Once the cycle of thought, emotion, and boiling blood takes place, it is best to keep silent until we are in control again. A good rule of thumb is to say nothing until the Lord has given us His thoughts and reactions to the problem.

Control 3: *Be slow to anger.*

The Greek word for anger is *orge*, which means "smoldering anger rooted in the fires of ego needs." Being "slow to anger" implies a period of prayer before expressing our feelings. This provides opportunity to review why we feel angry, and discover if our anger is really a cover for some other feelings we may need to address. Often our anger is a signal that we have not resolved a much larger issue.

Perhaps Tom's anger at the three bicycles in the driveway reflected his feeling that his children were irresponsible and that perhaps he was encouraging their actions by his willingness to provide material things. Or perhaps he felt that his wife, Cindy, was refusing to support him when disciplining the children, and he resented that.

Whatever the issue, anger over minutia often prevents our true feelings from surfacing so we can deal with the real issue.

When we find it difficult to contain our anger, we can try ignoring the child's behavior for the moment. Research indicates that when a behavior is ignored, that person will eventually stop or greatly reduce doing it. Psychologists call it "extinction" because it extinguishes the behavior. We can stand silently beside the child until the behavior subsides and then make our request known or acknowledge our feelings. Initially this method may actually increase the occurrence of the objectionable behavior as the child tries even harder to push our anger button. A word of caution: if this makes you furious . . . *stop!*

Or we can take time out. Anger can be healthy, provided it leads to some attempt to solve the cause of the anger. Therefore, time out may be exactly what most of us need in order to be "slow to anger." During our time out, we should try to accomplish three things: (1) contain our anger, (2) do some self-analysis, and (3) practice communicating without condemning.

Suppose you feel anger coming on. Try to find a quiet room—a place where you can pace slowly and deliberately. Then try to match your breathing to your steps. Inhale slowly through the nose and exhale slowly through the mouth. Continuing to breathe slower and slower, match your pacing to your breathing. For example, count 100 breaths, and then stop pacing and sit down and close your eyes. Imagine that you're alone on a deserted beach and you're listening to the surf. Experience the salt spray in your face and breathe deeply and slowly. After three to five minutes you should be in control.

Now spend a few more minutes analyzing the situation. Are there some aspects of this objectionable behavior that you had not thought of before? Stop feeling sorry for yourself, and refuse to sulk or crawl off into a shell. Determine the real cause of your anger. Next practice communicating your displeasure about the child's behavior without condemning. Only then are you ready to discipline your child with love.

If this seems like too much work, remember that anger can be addictive and you may be its victim. It is better to spend time alone in a quiet room than react violently and regret it the rest of your life. How I wish I had known about the quiet room concept when I was disciplining Mitch that day.

When we are angry with a child, we should ask ourselves, "How can I deal with this situation in a way that brings me closer to God and strengthens my relationship with my child?"

As we read the Gospels it is quite clear that Jesus was the master of His emotions. Jesus never lost His temper because of other people's reactions to Him, but He did become upset when they abused the Temple or misrepresented the Sabbath. When money changers became rich off other people's sins, Jesus became angry. When religious leaders accused Him of breaking the Sabbath commandment because He healed a withered hand on that day, Jesus became angry. But when they spat in His face, ridiculed Him publicly, and nailed Him to a cross, there was no anger in Him at all. Anger came only as a response to the neglect of human needs or the blasphemous use of religion to misrepresent God. "Man's anger" is far different from the "righteous life that God desires" (James 1:20, NIV).

In order to be righteous, we must be right with God. When we are angry with a child, we should ask ourselves, "How can I deal with this situation in a way that brings me closer to God and strengthens my relationship with my child?"

Two Greek words are of significance in being right with God. One word, *hamartia*, is translated "sin" and means to miss the mark. Whenever our actions cause us to miss the mark with our children, or create a separation between us, we are guilty of sin.

The second word, *prautes*, is usually translated "humility" or "meekness." This multifaceted word is not easy to define accurately. It applies to the mean between excessive anger and no anger. It implies a quality of control over the feelings and emotions. It refers to moderation in the expression of anger, in which reason controls expression and serenity is never lost. It refers to teachableness and receptivity to learning. It even refers to an animal that has been tamed to respond to the reins (commands) of its master. It is in humility that we should discipline our children.

So how can this work for you? How can you control your anger in such a way that you do not create relational problems (separation) for your children or yourself? Make Christ your Lord and Master. If He lives within you, then His attitude will control your emotions.

Christ will act as a lightning rod, grounding your negative emotions before they destroy you and those around you. He will intercept those disturbing thoughts that cause you to lose your temper with your children. Before the anger signal is sent to your limbic system, Jesus intercepts the message and breaks the destructive cycle.

Christ will act as a lightning rod, grounding your negative emotions before they destroy you and those around you. He will intercept those disturbing thoughts that cause you to lose your temper with your children. Before the anger signal is sent to your limbic system, Jesus intercepts the message and breaks the destructive cycle. You are given His perception and grace to respond and act as He would in that situation.

When you become one with Christ, He becomes the Master of your thoughts, actions, and reactions. With Jesus in charge, you can work to bring about constructive changes in your children rather than excusing your destructive reactions.

When Christ is in control, bicycles in the driveway, bread on the counter, and socks on the floor will not cause you to nag your children, making them angry and resentful. "Rather, [you will] bring them up with the loving discipline the Lord himself approves, with suggestions and godly advice" (Eph. 6:4, TLB).

Thought Questions

1. Reflect on the following statement: "Don't keep on scolding and nagging your children, making them angry and resentful" (Eph. 6:4, TLB). How might this statement apply to you?

2. Describe one of your pet peeves.

3. Recall a time when you repressed anger. Has it ever surfaced again? Explain.

CHAPTER 6

"Where Did You Learn That?"

(Teaching Values)

> *"The righteous man leads a blameless life; blessed are his children after him"* (Prov. 20:7, NIV).

According to Robert Fulghum, everything you really need to know in life you have learned by the time you finish kindergarten. Read the following list and see if you agree:

Share everything.

Play fair.

Don't hit people.

Put things back where you found them.

Clean up your own mess.

Don't take things that aren't yours.

Say you're sorry when you hurt somebody.

Wash your hands before you eat.

Flush.

Warm cookies and cold milk are good for you.

Live a balanced life.

Take a nap every afternoon.

When you go out into the world, watch out for traffic, hold hands, and stick together.

Be aware of wonder. Remember the little seed in the Styrofoam cup: The roots go down and the plant goes up and nobody knows how or why, but we are all like that.

Goldfish and hamsters and white mice and even the little seed in the Styrofoam cup—they all die. So do we.

Remember the Dick-and-Jane books and the first word you learned—the biggest word of all—LOOK (*All I Really Need To Know I Learned in Kindergarten*, pp. 4, 5).

He's right, isn't he? We learned everything, that is, except God! That seems to be the one important value left out. The golden rule, love, basic sanitation, ecology, politics, equality, sane living—it's all there except for God.

Perhaps the earliest lessons are truly those that stay with us for a lifetime. Wouldn't it be nice if the whole world had chocolate chip cookies and milk every day about 3:00 p.m., and then all of us would lie down with our blankies for a nap? Isn't it sad that some of those early lessons fall away with the responsibilities and mad rush of adulthood?

An interesting survey appeared in *USA Today*. The information was taken from a newsletter at the University of Michigan. Identical surveys of mothers were taken more than 60 years apart to determine the values they felt were important.

	1924			1988	
Loyalty to Church:	50%		Independence:	76%	
Strict Obedience:	45%		Tolerance:	47%	
Independence:	25%		Loyalty to Church:	22%	
Tolerance:	6%		Strict Obedience:	17%	

Perhaps this survey reveals why Fulghum left God out of his list of important things to know. Values have changed dramatically in the past 60 years. In a recent survey only 50 percent of 18- to 24-year-olds honestly felt they received a strong moral foundation from their parents. However, 60 percent of adults ages 25 to 60 and 78 percent of those 65 or older credited their parents with providing them with a strong moral foundation (Patterson and Kim, *The Day America Told the Truth*, p. 62).

An even more depressing statistic is that 91 percent of Americans tell lies on a regular basis (*ibid.*, p. 45).

There seems to be no moral consensus at all in the 1990s. All have become a law unto themselves. Personal moral codes are more important than traditional values or God's commandments. This generation has written a new set of personal commandments as it enters the next millennium.

1. I don't see the point in observing the Sabbath (77 percent).

2. I will steal from those who won't really miss it (74 percent).

3. I will lie when it suits me, so long as it doesn't cause any real damage (64 percent).

4. I will drink and drive if I feel that I can handle it. I know my limit (56 percent).

5. I will cheat on my spouse—after all, given the chance, he or she will do the same (53 percent).

6. I will procrastinate at work and do absolutely nothing for one full day in every five. It's standard operating procedure (50 percent).

7. I will use recreational drugs (41 percent).

8. I will cheat on my taxes—to a point (30 percent).

9. I will put my lover at risk of disease. I sleep around a bit, but who doesn't (31 percent)?

10. Technically, I may have committed date rape, but I know that she wanted it (20 percent have been date-raped) (*ibid.*, pp. 25, 26).

When Roger and Peggy Dudley surveyed a random sampling of Seventh-day Adventist parents and young people concerning their values and standards (*Ministry*, April 1985), they found that parents were basically more traditional than young people (which was to be expected). However, they discovered that the typical Seventh-day Adventist family still supports many traditional values even while their standards on marriage, family, and social purity are in a state of transition and in danger of being lost.

From their survey the Dudleys concluded that Seventh-day Adventist schools do not significantly alter values and that legalistic preaching was equally ineffective. Perhaps this is a direct result of what is *not* being taught at home.

Teachers today are often more concerned with damaging a student's psyche than reinforcing values. One young man had a notation on his report card that read: "Creative use of visual aids." Unable to determine exactly what that meant, the father called the teacher and inquired, "What does 'creative use of visual aids' mean?"

"Oh," replied the teacher, "that means he copies from the kid in the next seat."

"Some have no firmness of character. Their plans and purposes have no definite form and consistency. They are of but little practical use in the world. . . . We must have moral backbone, an integrity that cannot be flattered, bribed, or terrified" (Ellen G. White, *The Ministry of Healing*, p. 498).

How can we parents meet this challenge? How do we instill moral backbone in our children? How do we teach them unwavering integrity? The Bible emphatically places this responsibility upon the parents: "These commandments that I give you today are to be upon your hearts. Impress them on your children. Talk about them when you sit at home and when you walk along the road, when you lie down and when you get up. Tie them as symbols on your hands and bind them on your foreheads. Write them on the doorframes of your houses and on your gates" (Deut. 6:6-9, NIV).

Home is God's intended place for teaching values. We cannot fault the school system or the church. God places the responsibility squarely on the shoulders of parents. It is in the context of the home that values are passed on.

Home is God's intended place for teaching values. We cannot fault the school system or the church. God places the responsibility squarely on the shoulders of parents. It is in the context of the home that values are passed on.

The 6-year-old son of an accountant for a large corporation was used to hearing large sums of money mentioned at the dinner table. Not to be outdone, he came racing into the house one evening and announced to his father, "I just sold the dog for $10,000."

"Sold the dog!" exclaimed the father. "What are you talking about? Where's the money?"

"Oh, I didn't get any money," replied the boy proudly. "It was a trade. I got two $5,000 cats for him!"

Values are more *caught* than taught. What our children hear and see in the home they tend to mimic. Rosalie Elliot, an 11-year-old from South Carolina, was in the fourth round of a national spelling contest in Washington, D.C. The word she drew was "avowal." In her soft Southern accent she slowly spelled it out. But the judges could not decide if she had used an "a" or an "e" for the next-to-the-last letter.

The tape was replayed several times, but the judges still could not decide. Finally they asked the one person in the auditorium who knew which vowel she had used—Rosalie. By this time Rosalie had heard the correct spelling whispered many times by the other contestants while the judges were reviewing the tape. But when asked by the judges, she replied without hesitation, "I misspelled the word," and walked off the stage.

The entire audience came to its feet and applauded the integrity of Rosalie. More than 50 reporters were in attendance, and one remarked that the judges had certainly put a heavy burden on an 11-year-old. Did they? Or should we be disappointed because so many doubted that Rosalie would do the right thing?

In order to teach values and integrity, parents must be in control. It may be necessary to reaffirm from time to time, "I am the parent!" Experts say that parents who are comfortable as adult authority figures find it easiest to teach values. Values must be taught repeatedly because children under the age of 7 are likely to find it difficult to generalize from one instance to another. So parents must teach the same lessons again and again, in differing circumstances, in order for small children to understand the general principle.

Values must be taught repeatedly because children under the age of 7 are likely to find it difficult to generalize from one instance to another. So parents must teach the same lessons again and again, in differing circumstances, in order for small children to understand the general principle.

One way that parents can remain in control is to allow children choices in another area. It is possible to monitor the television without preaching. For instance, if parents want to limit television viewing or if an objectionable program is being aired, they might decide to keep the TV off after dinner, while involving their children in another activity. It is important for parents to fill children's time, not just monitor it. They should use this time to do something special with their children.

This type of "give and take" strategy also works well with teenagers. We parents should listen carefully to our teenagers and then share our views on the subject. It is possible that both the adults and the teens will learn something from the exchange. The bottom line is to allow our teens to make decisions that do not conflict with our (and hopefully their) values.

It is important for parents to define the values they wish to teach children—before they begin teaching. We can make a list and keep it handy for reference. It might include such things as kindness, fairness, tolerance, integrity, courtesy, generosity, responsibility, self-respect, etc. (The value of knowing God is covered in another chapter, but should be first on any list.) By defining the values we feel are important, we can monitor our own behavior as we try to teach our children.

Children who feel loved tend to be friendly, generous, and affectionate. Their teachers and peers judge them as being honest, responsible, and loyal.

We should always teach values with *love*. It is important for us to cuddle and touch young children. We should talk soothingly and reassuringly except when we want a behavior change. Children must be able to discern by our different tone that we are requesting a change in behavior. As soon as the unwanted behavior has stopped, we can return to a soothing, reassuring tone. Children quickly learn that their parents are in control and still love them even when disappointed with their behavior.

For older children, we can show our affection by taking genuine interest and pleasure in their company. We can try to understand their goals and desires. We can rejoice in their successes and comfort them and sympathize with them during their failures.

One youngster brought home a very poor report card, and his mother asked, "What have you to say about this?"

"Well, one thing's for sure," replied the boy. "You know I'm not cheating!"

Children who feel loved tend to be friendly, generous, and affectionate. Their teachers and peers judge them as being honest, responsible, and loyal.

However, children who feel rejected tend to be aggressive and unloving. Which characteristics do we want our children to possess for the rest of their lives?

Using questions is an effective way to teach children right from wrong. We can help our children establish their own values by teaching them to ask the following questions:

> Does this activity make me feel happy?
> Does it accomplish the job I've set out to do?
> Does it make others happy?
> Would I do it this way if Jesus were here with me?
> Am I proud of what I am doing?
> Would I do it this way again?

The use of these questions will also help children develop empathy, another important value. Our teaching children to think about the needs and feelings of others will emphasize the values we want them to catch. And we should not feel discouraged if our children do not appear empathetic until they

Empathy provides a solid foundation upon which children can base all moral decisions. Therefore, it is important for parents to nurture empathy at every opportunity, regardless of the child's age.

are in kindergarten. Most children are basically egocentric and truly unable to consider others before age 4. Even good decisions at an early age may have more to do with earning a reward than being empathetic or nice. Obviously the maturity of children varies greatly, along with their temperament and culture.

Empathy provides a solid foundation upon which children can base all moral decisions. Therefore, it is important for parents to nurture empathy at every opportunity, regardless of the child's age. Empathy is developed by being honest with children.

In one experiment researchers specifically instructed children not to look at a specified toy. They found that two thirds of 3-year-old children who had peeked lied about it. By the age of 7, 90 percent of those who peeked lied to cover it up.

It is vital that parents not set up their children to lie. We should avoid making accusations or attempting to entrap them. Instead of saying "Did you take some cookies without asking me?" we can say "I realize you must be hungry, but please do not take any cookies without asking me."

When we tell them what we already know, children can admit the wrong and clearly see that we know what they have done.

If we wish to teach values in the home, it is necessary for us parents to clarify family rules. Rather than yelling "How many times do I have to tell you not to interrupt me when I'm talking on the phone?" we can try saying "Don't interrupt me when I'm talking on the phone because it is impolite to the person with whom I'm speaking." Rather than shouting "Why can't you ever listen? I've told you a thousand times not to run in the apartment!" we can try saying "Don't run in the apartment because it is inconsiderate to our downstairs neighbors."

Responsibility is an important teaching tool for values' education. Unless children learn to be responsible for their actions, the values we teach will always belong to us rather than to the children.

Role playing is another innovative way of teaching values to children. It can be especially helpful if we reverse roles and let the children play the parents. Often children will use the same phrases as their parents when under stress in role playing. "Wait just a minute! I can't listen to both of you at once" may be a child's plea. This approach also helps children develop empathy.

Responsibility is an important teaching tool for values' education. Unless children learn to be responsible for their actions, the values we teach will always belong to us rather than to the children.

One little boy, obviously operating on his parents' value system, was asked to define conscience. His answer was simply, "Something that makes me tell my mother before my sister does."

Learning to be responsible for personal choices is one of the primary lessons in values' education. We should encourage children to keep their commitments. If we assign specific household chores to them, we can reward them when they have completed these chores and can allow them to suffer the consequences when they have not. If we promise the reward of a frozen yogurt at the mall on Sunday for taking out the trash each night, then we should not provide it if the trash was not taken out each night. However, the rest of the family members should receive their reward for completing their tasks. It does not take too many missed yogurts for children to learn the lesson of personal choices.

Peer pressure will be especially difficult for children who have not learned to be responsible for their own choices. We parents should never accept "He made me do it" as an excuse. Children must learn to take responsibility for their own actions. If a child throws a toy during a tantrum, we can tell him or her "We don't throw things. Pick it up!" If he or she throws it again, we should impose a time out. (See the chapter on discipline.)

Personal choices made in childhood will have a more serious impact later in life. The choices then will involve drugs, alcohol, sex, stealing, and other undesirable acts. Children who have not taken personal responsibility for their actions with toys will probably blame someone else for their use of drugs later.

In learning to take personal responsibility for their choices, children must face the music. They must face the people whom they have wronged, or try to correct the problem their actions have created. This is a difficult task, but it will be less difficult to do as an adult if it has been properly learned as a child. This means that, as parents, we too must be willing to face the music when we have acted in ways that seemingly contradict our values.

I think of one Seventh-day Adventist mother who had taught her child not to do any shopping on Sabbath. One Sabbath the mother went to the drugstore to fill a prescription for a sick neighbor. Later, indignant as only a 6-year-old can be, the child said, "I thought we weren't supposed to go shopping on Sabbath!"

The mother's first impulse was anger, but then she realized that her daughter was responding to the values she had been taught. So the mother used this occasion to explain what Jesus meant when He spoke about the ox in the ditch. Another lesson in values learned!

Understanding children's behavior may be more important than the behavior itself. For example, if a child is caught stealing, he or she may reveal the real motives by what is done with the loot. If the child shows it to no one, he or she probably wants it for its own sake. If the child shows it to friends, he or she may be seeking their approval. If the child shows it to you or another adult, he or she undoubtedly is seeking help. Once you understand the reason for the behavior, you will often find it easier to correct.

The old adage "Monkey see, monkey do" is appropriate for teaching values. Children typically model behavior that they have seen somewhere else—usually at home.

Children copy both good and bad behavior. If they hear a parent using four-letter words, they will try them out at school, on their friends, or at a dinner party. There is never a time when parents are not teaching their children. Whatever we do not want our children to do in public, we should also refrain from doing in private.

Ruby Bridges, a Black 6-year-old, was among the first to enter a racially segregated school during the 1950s. A crowd was shouting as usual. A woman spat at Ruby but missed; Ruby smiled at her. A man shook his fist at her; Ruby smiled at him. Do you know what she told one of the marshals? She said that she prayed for those people, the ones in that mob, every night before she went to sleep. At the age of 6, Ruby was acting more mature and Christlike than most of the adults in the crowd. She simply modeled the behavior of her parents. Ruby had caught the values her parents had been modeling throughout her six years.

There is never a time when parents are not teaching their children. Whatever we do not want our children to do in public, we should also refrain from doing in private.

When parents work outside the home, day care is an important consideration. Parents should know what the baby-sitter is teaching their children. Does she watch the afternoon soaps while baby-sitting? What type of language does she use in the home? It would be desirable for parents to develop their own list of "bottom line" questions and have it handy for the initial interview. The day-care person becomes an important role model for the children overseen.

Another important influence upon children's value systems is the media. Their subtle influence is constantly bombarding the values of children.

Most younger children can recite their favorite commercials from memory. From the latest toy to the latest jeans, the media helps determine values.

Paul seemed to have special insight into our modern media programming when he wrote to the church in Rome: "For although they knew God, they neither glorified him as God nor gave thanks to him, but their thinking became futile and their foolish hearts were darkened. Although they claimed to be wise, they became fools. . . . Therefore God gave them over in the sinful desires of their hearts to sexual impurity for the degrading of their bodies with one another. They exchanged the truth of God for a lie" (Rom. 1:21-25, NIV).

The influence of the mass media upon parents and children is changing the values of a whole generation. A teacher was trying to impress upon her students the importance of being honest. "Suppose you found a briefcase with $1 million in it. What would you do?"

Immediately Johnny raised his hand and replied, "If it belonged to a poor family I'd return it."

Isn't it sad that honesty applies to only the poor today? Evidently taking something from the rich is not really stealing. Robin Hood now steals from Uncle Sam and large corporations because they are "rich." Some parents today want to teach honesty to their children but do not practice it in their daily life. In fact, many would think that the person who turned in $1 million was some kind of nut.

Helping our children take responsibility for their thoughts is an essential part of parenting.

Even our friends and relatives have a subtle influence upon our children's value systems. Think about some of the remarks you have heard them make and their hidden values:

"What a sharp-looking outfit she has on!" (emphasis on the latest style)

"What a beautiful child!" (emphasis on physical appearance)

"He can't count yet? My son is reading already!" (emphasis on gifted development and intelligence)

"He doesn't have to share his candy if he doesn't want to." (emphasis on selfishness)

Thus far we have explored techniques for teaching children values. However, there must be a source. What is this source? What is the foundation for your value system? Is it the community? society? the country in which you live? God's Word? Who is the source of your values? The Bible clearly defines a value system for both the family and community. Notice God's love lyrics (the Ten Commandments), which are the basic values for life.

1. Love God.
2. Love God more than things.
3. Love the name of God.
4. Love God's Sabbath day.
5. Love your father and mother.
6. Love human life.
7. Love your body.
8. Love honesty.
9. Love truthfulness.
10. Love what God gives you.

Children are naturally legalistic and often hide their real feelings while acting out the letter of the law.

As we teach these basic life values to our children, it would be beneficial to have them memorize Jesus' summation. They may find His synopsis easier to understand. " 'Love the Lord your God with all your heart, soul, and mind.' This is the first and greatest commandment. The second most important is similar: 'Love your neighbor as much as you love yourself.' All the other commandments and all the demands of the prophets stem from these two laws and are fulfilled if you obey them. Keep only these and you will find that you are obeying all the others" (Matt. 22:37-40, TLB).

Jesus reminds us that our thoughts often speak louder than our words or actions. Children are naturally legalistic and often hide their real feelings while acting out the letter of the law. In His sermon on the mount, Jesus made it quite clear that we are also responsible for our thoughts (see Matt. 5-6). Helping our children take responsibility for their thoughts is an essential part of parenting.

How can we teach biblical values to our children? Church attendance is a good beginning. We parents may want to check out the children's divisions for ourselves. We cannot assume that our children will learn about the values of loving God and loving others. Also, we can learn to speak positively about the pastor even if we dislike his preaching style. We can look for the best in his most boring sermon. In so doing, we will find it easier to control our own thoughts as well.

We can read Bible stories with the family and discuss their meaning. What lessons are to be learned from each story? We can try to remember a time in our own experience that is similar. We can ask our children to make it a modern-day parable and tell it back to us in their own words.

We should pray with our children daily. When children learn to talk to God about everything, they will find it easier to control their thoughts. It is important that we parents also talk to God as a friend if we want our children to trust and love their Creator.

We can demonstrate love in action by doing kind deeds for our neighbors. We should involve our children as much as possible so that they too can experience the "warm fuzzies" of sharing.

Values are more the product of attitude than aptitude. Learning to do the right things is not nearly as important as learning to think the right thoughts.

We can compliment the character qualities in our children rather than the physical attributes. A healthy self-esteem is formed from within and should not be based on something over which the children have little or no control (for example, physical attributes).

When we disagree with someone in authority, we can do it respectfully. Whether it be the boss, an elected official, or our pastor, we should disagree in respectful tones and words.

Even we parents can learn to say "I'm sorry" when we are wrong. This teaches children the importance of forgiveness and models how it is to be used.

Values are more the product of attitude than aptitude. Learning to do the right things is not nearly as important as learning to think the right thoughts. "First clean the inside of the cup and dish, and then the outside also will be clean. . . . You are like whitewashed tombs, which look beautiful on the outside but on the inside are full of dead men's bones and everything unclean" (Matt. 23:26, 27, NIV).

The do's and don'ts that are often regarded as teaching values are woefully insufficient. Teaching children values is more than strict obedience. It is attitude development.

The most effective way we parents can teach values to our children is to live them ourselves. As we model our personal values, we will also be modeling something about God—especially for our younger children. Therefore, we must take our modeling seriously.

The parents of an 8-year-old boy took their modeling seriously, and this letter is the result. As this 8-year-old attempts to describe God, he reveals the values he has been taught. (A misspelled word is purposely left uncorrected.)

"One of God's main jobs is making people. He makes these to put in place of the ones that die so there will be enough people to take care of things here on earth. He doesn't make grown-ups. Just babies. I think because they are smaller and easier to make. That way He doesn't have to take up His valuable time teaching them to talk and walk. He can just leave that up to the mothers and fathers. I think it works out pretty good.

"God's second most important job is listening to prayers. An awful lot of this goes on, as some people, like preachers and things, pray other times besides bedtime. God doesn't have time to listen to the radio or TV on account of this. As He hears everything, not only prayers, there must be a terrible lot of noise going into His ears unless He has thought of a way to turn it off.

"God sees everything and hears everything and is everywhere. Which keeps Him pretty busy. So you shouldn't go wasting His time by going over your parents' head and asking for something they said you couldn't have.

"Atheists are people who don't believe in God. I don't think there are any in Chula Vista. At least there aren't any who come to our church.

"Jesus is God's Son. He used to do all the hard work like walking on water and doing miracles and trying to teach people about God who didn't want to learn. They finally got tired of Him preaching to them and they cursified [not too far from the truth!] Him. But He was good and kind like His Father, and He told His Father that they didn't know what they were doing and to forgive them and God said OK. His Dad (God) appreciated everything He had done and all His hard work on earth, so He told Him He didn't have to go on the road anymore. He could stay in heaven. So He did. And now He helps His

Dad out by listening to prayers and seeing which things are important for God to take care of and which ones He can take care of Himself without bothering God about. Like a secretary—only more important, of course. You can pray anytime you want and They are sure to hear you because They've got it worked out so one of Them is on duty all the time.

"You should always go to church because it makes God happy, and if there's anybody you want to make happy, it's God! Don't skip church to do something you think will be more fun, like going to the beach. That is wrong. And besides, the sun doesn't come out at the beach until noon, anyway.

"If you don't believe in God, besides being an atheist, you will be very lonely, because your parents can't go everywhere with you like to camp, but God can. It's good to know He's around when you're scared of the dark or when you can't swim very good and you get thrown in the real deep water by big kids. But you shouldn't just always think of what God can do for you. I figure God put me here and He can take me back anytime He pleases. And that's why I believe in God" (Danny Dutton, age 8, Chula Vista, California).

Thought Questions

1. What was one of the earliest lessons you learned as a child? How has it affected your parenting style?

2. Can you list five moral values that you would die for? If not, are there any you would die for?

3. Since children are naturally legalists and often hide their true feelings while acting out the letter of the law, how can you be certain that your children understand and accept your value system?

CHAPTER 7

"Who Told You Sex Was Dirty?"

(Teaching Your Child About Sex)

> *"So God created man in his own image, in the image of God he created him; male and female he created them. God blessed them and said to them, 'Be fruitful and increase in number.' . . . God saw all that he had made, and it was very good"* (Gen. 1:27-31, NIV).

Many parents today wonder when—or if—they should begin teaching their children about sex and its proper place in the life of a Christian. This can be a difficult decision in the life of any parent. How do we begin to teach our children what God had in mind when He created us male and female? How do we get past the misinformation that our parents may have shared with us? How do we teach sexuality in a nation in which almost one third of all married Americans (31 percent) have had or are now having an affair? In addition, almost two thirds of those having an affair think there's nothing morally wrong with it (Patterson and Kim, *The Day America Told the Truth*, pp. 94, 95).

Our children are starting to have sexual relations far earlier than any previous generation in our nation. One in five children now loses his or her virginity before the age of 13 (*ibid.*, p. 100).

Current statistics indicate that teenage pregnancies cost our nation more than $16 billion a year and cause a tremendous rate of dropout in our schools. In fact, 70 percent of teenage mothers under age 15 will drop out of school, creating a burden upon themselves, their family, and their society.

Why are so many teenage girls becoming pregnant during this period of sexual enlightenment? Perhaps it is because sex seldom takes its rightful place in a modern relationship, but is often the only reason for the relationship.

In Washington, D.C., the average teenager defines a long-term relationship as one that lasts from three weeks to three months (*Psychology Today*, January/February 1989, p. 10). During that brief period of time sex is expected to play an important role. If it does not, a couple runs the risk of ridicule and peer pressure.

There is no doubt that sexual mores have changed during the past 20 years. The baby-boomer generation ended the double standard as it applied to virginity at marriage. In previous generations twice as many women as men came to the altar as virgins. Today they are within 10 percentage points of each other—25 percent men versus 34 percent women (*The Day America Told the Truth*, p. 101).

Among the current baby-buster generation almost two thirds lost their virginity by the age of 16. Yet only 10 percent of them gave love as their reason for having sex. The overwhelming reason for early sex among the baby busters is peer pressure without any effective counterforce from parents or schools.

However, baby boomers married later than any previous generation, so the statistics included men and women in their 20s and 30s. Among the current baby-buster generation almost two thirds lost their virginity by the age of 16. Yet only 10 percent of them gave love as their reason for having sex. The overwhelming reason for early sex among the baby busters is peer pressure without any effective counterforce from parents or schools (*ibid.*, p. 102).

Children today are growing up in an environment in which everyone's value system is supported. If you're a virgin, that's fine. If you're sexually active, that's fine. If you're gay, that's fine. If your parent sleeps around, that's fine.

Today at a birthday party you are likely to find a fourth-grade girl wearing tight pants, a designer blouse, and dangling earrings, while gyrating to hard rock music with words that insist the singer wants sex—*your* sex—and insists that he or she wants your body. Most girls age 9 to 11 use nail polish. By the age 13 they will add perfume, lipstick, blush, and eye shadow. By the time she enters her teen years, the average girl will be spending more than $250 a year on adult cosmetics, all with parental approval and even delight (*ibid.*, p. 103).

Everything is happening so fast today. How can we parents make sense of it all? The late Dr. Charles Wittschiebe used an interesting simile to illustrate the difficulty of controlling sex in a relationship. "Sex is like a horse, a spirited horse. You don't want him to throw you, but you don't want to lock him in the barn or drug him. He's there to be ridden, controlled, and enjoyed. Abusing him, misusing him, losing control, does away with the fun of having him" (*Teens and Love and Sex*, p. 82).

It is important for us parents to teach our children at an early age about that spirited steed. If we wait until our children are 9, we may be too late! With one out of five children losing his or her virginity by age 13, we parents no longer have the option of waiting to discuss sexuality until our children are teenagers. Perhaps we never have, although some of us seemingly have ignored this parental responsibility entirely.

"Biological attraction should furnish the electricity for the relationship, but it should not be allowed to become so overpowering that it short-circuits the entire relationship."

The purpose of this chapter is not to outline home sex education in its entirety. There are many quality Christian books available that cover the subject quite well. I am concerned about parents helping their children cope with intense feelings they do not understand and find very difficult to control. As Dr. Wittschiebe remarked: "Biological attraction should furnish the electricity for the relationship, but it should not be allowed to become so overpowering that it short-circuits the entire relationship" (*Teens and Love and Sex*, p. 37).

When our children approach puberty, we might begin by reviewing with them the powerful changes they are about to experience. If we can recall, we can share with them how we felt at that age. Most of us will have several vivid recollections permanently engraved in our book of memories. At first we may not feel comfortable talking with them about our own fears and sexual misinformation when we approached our teen years.

If you are a father, you might admit to your son how worried you were in class when an unexpected erection occurred just as the teacher called upon you to give an impromptu presentation at the front of the room. Or possibly how your first nocturnal emission left you feeling guilty and confused about both your feelings and the stain on the bed sheets.

Perhaps you can recall some of the locker room bravado that was passed off as sexual experience. How none of the guys would admit to being a virgin, even though most of them probably were. Such candid conversation may be uncomfortable for you, but it can be very reassuring to your son. It will give him courage to ignore his peer pressure if you explain to him that your generation still shares some of these same mistaken ideas concerning manhood. Assure your teen that being a man has nothing to do with the locker room use of crude jokes, coarse language, and bragging about "scoring."

If you're a mother, you may recall with your daughter your early sexual urges or related happenings. Maybe you can remember a specific time when you first became interested in boys. While your sex drive probably awakened slowly over a period of years, it is important to share such information with your daughter. Assure her that she is perfectly normal if she has developed a crush on a male teacher. Explain to her how her emotions and sex drive change with menstruation. You may be embarrassed to admit it if you were not psychologically (or perhaps even physiologically) prepared for your first period.

Explain to her that a strong sex drive seems to appear in the male almost overnight, whereas the female enjoys a more gradual curve from preadolescence through her early 20s. You might even tell about some pajama parties during which all your friends "stayed over" at a friend's house and talked about boys all night. Perhaps you might even reveal your own feelings when a boy kissed you for the first time, or at the first fumbling attempts of a boy to fondle your breasts.

Some of you may be staring at this page in disbelief or even disgust. How can a Christian talk about such things? If these are your thoughts, you probably hold the view that sex is dirty or sinful. Some psychologists believe we may have received that mistaken concept as the result of early toilet training. The scenario goes something like this: Little Mary is busy playing with the other children and does not want to take time out to go to the bathroom. She plays too long and soon finds she has relieved herself in her clothes.

Mother walks by and notices what is happening. "What in the world are you doing?" Mother yells. "Now look what you have done! You're a *dirty* little girl. Shame on you!" Mother compounds these words by marching Mary into the bathroom to get cleaned up.

One can begin to understand the association of sex organs with being dirty.

Perhaps it was little Freddy who was always willing to take a dare. Some of the children dared him to pull down his pants. Just as he accepts this challenge, Father walks by.

"Freddy, get those pants back up this instant! I can't believe what I'm seeing. What's the matter with you, anyway? You're a *dirty* little boy."

Children are often taught that the sex organs are shameful and dirty, when in fact the problem is merely one of proper social graces in a particular society. Actually, the sex organs are very clean. Both the male penis and female urethra discharge urine, which is a sterile waste product, from our body. Actually, both male and female sex organs are much cleaner than the mouth.

It is important for us to teach young children that sex organs are covered *not* because they are dirty, but because they are private.

So it is important for us to teach young children that sex organs are covered *not* because they are dirty, but because they are private. Our society considers them to be our personal private parts, and it is not considered good manners to display them in public. In addition, sexual sins are the result of the mind, not the sex organs. The sex organs merely respond to the mind's instructions. If we want to cover something in shame, perhaps it should be the head, where sexual sin originates.

Often when parents catch children masturbating or "playing doctor" with other children, their reaction causes the children to feel dirty. It is little wonder that at a very early age children make the association that their sexual organs are dirty.

As a child you may have unwittingly interrupted your parents while they were having sex. Perhaps their startled reaction and physical position may have given you the impression that sex was dirty or awful. After all, with such moaning and physical pounding, something bad must have been happening. If you also happened to catch a glimpse of pornographic pictures or magazines that some kid secretively brought to school, you may have concluded that sex was at least lewd if not downright filthy. It is, of course, in that context. This is far from what God had in mind when He created us male and female. Sin has resulted in the exploitation of all natural acts, including sex.

Sometimes we parents even use Scripture to convince our children that sex is sinful and dirty. Let me review a few of the favorites, using the New International Version:

"The body is not meant for sexual immorality, but for the Lord, and the Lord for the body" (1 Cor. 6:13).

"I am afraid that when I come again my God will humble me before you, and I will be grieved over many who have sinned earlier and have not repented of the impurity, sexual sin and debauchery in which they have indulged" (2 Cor. 12:21).

"The acts of the sinful nature are obvious: sexual immorality, impurity and debauchery" (Gal. 5:19).

In addition, sexual sins are the result of the mind, not the sex organs. The sex organs merely respond to the mind's instructions. If we want to cover something in shame, perhaps it should be the head, where sexual sin originates.

"But among you there must not be even a hint of sexual immorality, or of any kind of impurity, or of greed, because these are improper for God's holy people" (Eph. 5:3).

"Put to death, therefore, whatever belongs to your earthly nature: sexual immorality, impurity, lust, evil desires and greed, which is idolatry" (Col. 3:5).

"It is God's will that you should be sanctified; that you should avoid sexual immorality; that each of you should learn to control his own body in a way that is holy and honorable, not in passionate lust like the heathen, who do not know God" (1 Thess. 4:3-5).

These hard-hitting texts strike at the heart of our sinful nature.

However, unless these texts are given within the context of sex as a gift from God, children may feel that the Bible also views sex as dirty or sinful. We need to explain to our children that the reason God condemns sex outside of marriage is because it is a gift too precious to be wasted. The gift of sex is meant to be given to one's permanent mate, not a passing acquaintance.

One Christian author notes: "It is significant that among the mammals, only the human female is capable of enjoying sexual orgasm as well as the male. It is recognized that this experience binds a woman to her partner emotionally as well as physically. The fact that both the human male and female can share together in the pleasure of sexual intercourse indicates that God intended marital sex to be enjoyed by both partners" (Samuele Bacchiocchi, *The Marriage Covenant*, p. 75).

The Song of Songs portrays a beautiful celebration of sexual love between a bride and bridegroom. Paul compares the relationship of God and His church to the sexual relationship of a husband and wife. Scripture offers a very positive view concerning the gift of sex.

The Song of Songs portrays a beautiful celebration of sexual love between a bride and bridegroom. Paul compares the relationship of God and His church to the sexual relationship of a husband and wife. Scripture offers a very positive view concerning the gift of sex. It is also adamant that this gift is to be reserved for the marriage relationship.

Sometimes young people view sex like the forbidden tree in the Garden of Eden. Since it is so pleasant to look upon, why not try it? Just as the tree in the garden referred to a relationship between God and the first couple, so sex refers to a relationship between husband and wife. As Eve ate of the fruit, so some teens engage in premarital sex to gain knowledge. But a little knowledge (especially with the possibility of AIDS) can be deadly. In fact, young people often have just enough knowledge about sex to get into deep trouble.

In his book *Too Close Too Soon*, Jim Talley offers some interesting insights. "Infatuation, sexual attraction, and romantic attachment make people feel so good in the presence of the object of those emotions that the experience is labeled 'true love' and expected to last forever. Yet true love is so much more than feelings. It is the choice to invest in the life of a beloved, not only when it feels good but also when it doesn't" (pp. 14, 15).

Teaching children the difference between infatuation and love is a good beginning. Perhaps the simplest way to explain the difference is that we *fall* into infatuation but *grow* into love. In other words, it takes time for love to blossom, but infatuation reaches its maturity almost overnight. Usually relationships of three to six months are based on infatuation, not love. It takes time for love to grow and mature to the point where it is recognizable. Infatuation often meets an immature or emotional need such as a low self-image or problems in a parent-child relationship. Flattery is a strong indication that a relationship is based on infatuation rather than love.

Infatuation is time-consuming and almost overwhelming. Those involved can think of little else. Interest in God, church attendance, or being with other close friends is secondary if present at all. Infatuation, often mistaken for love by both children and parents, results in broken relationships, family problems, and teenage mothers. Unfortunately, many parents themselves married while under the ecstasy of infatuation rather than waiting for the permanency of love.

> **We *fall* into infatuation but *grow* into love. In other words, it takes time for love to blossom, but infatuation reaches its maturity almost overnight.**

When our children go through their first puppy love experience, we have an excellent opportunity to explain what is happening to their emotions. We might even admit that we did not always understand the difference between infatuation and love. Had we been given this insight, perhaps our own childhood and dating days might have been different. We might explain how we coped with sexual urges. We can assure our children that the intense emotions they now feel are perfectly normal and controllable. Remaining a virgin until marriage is a precious gift (and God's plan) for our children to bring to the marriage relationship.

We should inform our children that premarital sex makes a statement about their partner that is not very flattering. Infatuation leads them to believe that because they love this person so much, sex must be OK. But what if it isn't really love? What if it is temporary infatuation and never grows into love? What if it is just plain, old-fashioned, selfish lust? What if they contract venereal disease? What if they contract AIDS? What if pregnancy occurs? What if they fall out of love? What if? What if? What if? Without a permanent commitment in marriage, they are actually robbing their partner of their most precious gift and putting themselves in danger. Unless they are fully prepared to take all the risks and responsibilities inherent in the sex act, they are merely using the other person to satisfy their own personal needs. Lust is a user.

However, even after making all these points, parents should not assume that their children will refrain from sex. Statistics indicate that by the age of 13, the majority of males have engaged in sex and by the age of 15 so have the majority of females. A study at Indiana University concludes that to tell boys not to have sex because they will feel bad about it is ludicrous, even though this is often true for girls (*USA Today*, Jan. 16, 1989).

Another survey indicates that four out of five teenage boys indicated that morality was very important to them (*Parade*, Dec. 12, 1988). Such dichotomy often creates tremendous inner tension in both male and female teens.

The following comments, paraphrased from Charles Wittschiebe, should help us parents prepare to communicate about sexual conduct with our children.

1. I [male] need to get some experience before marriage.

Your reply: What will this experience cost you and your future wife? It means you will miss out on sharing these special *firsts* with her. Chastity (that means reserving this gift for your eventual spouse) and ignorance are not the same thing. Reading will prepare you for your wedding night. Talking to a trusted married friend or to me, your parent, will prepare you. Sex education will prepare you. It is not necessary to *practice* since you have the rest of your life to make sex *perfect*.

As Wittschiebe says: "It's like enjoying a private garden instead of sharing a public park" (*Teens and Love and Sex*, p. 18).

2. We are already married in the sight of God.

Your reply: To become *one flesh* requires more than the sex act. Such a relationship implies a lifelong commitment (regardless of what some adults are doing today) made with a public declaration. There is much more to marriage than a ceremony. That only gives opportunity for a public declaration in the presence of witnesses. As one of my favorite writers admonishes: Marriage is "the work of the afteryears" and "a school from which [those who marry] are never in this life to be graduated" (*The Adventist Home*, p. 105).

3. Sex is the true wedding for those who really love each other.

Your reply: There is a valid reason our society requires certificates of marriage and some form of public expression. Such requirements force the individuals to count the cost of the commitment they are about to make. Marriage is more than sex. It is a commitment that two individuals make to each other in the presence of witnesses and verified with legal documents. In biblical times, the marriage ceremony was the marriage feast. However, sex did not become a part of the relationship until after the public feast.

4. We're engaged; therefore, it's all right.

Your reply: Actually, long engagements can be more destructive than productive. It is one thing to be engaged long enough to plan properly together and get to know each other, but it is unwise to prolong such an engagement when there is a strong mutual attraction. The Bible offers the following warning about long engagements: "Now to the unmarried: . . . If they cannot control themselves, they should marry, for it is better to marry than to burn with passion" (1 Cor. 7:8, 9, NIV).

While lust and love both begin with the same letter and often the same feeling, they are vastly different. Lust invariably decreases over time and age, while love increases.

5. Sex indicates the true depth of our love for each other.

Your reply: This particular statement is usually (but not exclusively) offered by the male. It represents the most selfish form of love. Such conditional love (If you love me, you will . . .) is better referred to as selfish lust. Such a relationship ignores two major ingredients that are necessary for a meaningful relationship: character and integrity.

While lust and love both begin with the same letter and often the same feeling, they are vastly different. Lust invariably decreases over time and age, while love increases. Having premarital sex may indicate more your lack of character or integrity than love.

6. I [female] want to feel fulfilled as a woman.

Your reply: The argument often goes something like this: Isn't it better to test sex with my lover so I don't marry a klutz? Such an argument actually begs the question. If fulfillment (whatever that means) is all you are seeking in a relationship, then you are missing the whole concept of commitment. Counselors assure us that any couple can fulfill the other's needs if they truly try. Some may need added instruction and practice, but we all have a lifetime to work on our technique. Like anything else in life, sex should get better with practice, but if technique becomes the focal point of your relationship, you will probably be disappointed. After all, how many can give an Academy Award-winning performance every day?

7. I need to exercise my sexual muscles.

Your reply: Can you actually identify your sexual muscles? The best exercise for sexual muscles takes place in the mind, and is called self-control. Learning to control your response to sexual urges will make you a better lover when the time is right. One who cannot control urges is an addict, whether it be sex or drugs.

8. I need to be certain my partner does not have a sexual dysfunction.

Your reply: Actually, men or women with true sexual dysfunctions are rare. Even if they weren't, premarital sex is no guarantee that problems will not develop later. In fact, premarital sex may actually be the trigger that causes sexual dysfunction later in life. Sexual performance before marriage is absolutely no indication of sexual performance after marriage.

9. I need to feel loved and wanted.

Your reply: Are you perhaps substituting sex because there's a problem with *our* relationship? If you are, sex is not the answer to parent-teen problems. Would it be helpful if we talked about it or went for counseling?

10. I'm afraid I am gay.

Your reply: If you are going to gauge your sexual preference on your first sexual encounter (or near-miss), you may indeed be disappointed. Sex is seldom mind-blowing rapture the first, second, or even third time. This may cause you to doubt your sexual preference even more. Actually, sex with someone of the opposite sex is not a true indicator, in any event, since many gays are bisexual.

When all is said and done concerning sex, it would be much better if there was a lot more said and a lot less done!

In his book *No Wonder They Call Him the Savior*, Max Lucado relates a story that originally appeared in the Miami *Herald*.

"Judith Bucknell was homicide number 106 that year. She was killed on a steamy June 9 evening. Age: 38. Weight: 109 pounds. Stabbed seven times. Strangled. She kept a diary. Had she not kept this diary, perhaps the memory of her would have been buried with her body. But the diary exists, a painful epitaph to a lonely life. The correspondent made this comment about her writings: 'In her diaries Judy created a character and a voice. The character is herself, wistful, struggling, weary; the voice is yearning. Judith Bucknell has failed to connect; age 38, many lovers, much love offered, none returned.'

"Successful as a secretary, but a loser at love. Her diary was replete with entries such as the following: 'Where are the men with the flowers . . . and music? Where are the men who call and ask for a genuine, actual date? Where are the men who would like to share more than my bed, my booze, my food? . . . I would like to have in my life, once before I pass through my life, the kind of sexual relationship which is part of a loving relationship.'

When all is said and done concerning sex, it would be much better if there was a lot more said and a lot less done!

"She never did. Judy was not a prostitute. She was not on drugs or on welfare. She never went to jail. She was not a social outcast. She was respectable. She jogged. She hosted parties. She wore designer clothes and had an apartment that overlooked the bay. And she was very lonely. 'I see people together, and I'm so jealous I want to throw up. What about me! What about me!'

"Though she had many lovers (59 in 56 months), she had little love. 'Who is going to love Judy Bucknell?' the diary continues. 'I feel so old. Unloved. Unwanted. Abandoned. Used up. I want to cry and sleep forever.' "

We can assure our children that sex is not the answer to life's problems. It only seems to complicate the problems we already have. The answer to many of life's problems is found in a loving, committed relationship. Unfortunately, many adults have not yet experienced a genuine commitment, even though they happen to be married. Therefore, they have great difficulty trying to reassure their children that relationships can work. Because there is no substitute for parental example, it might be well to reread this chapter and see if it also applies to you.

Thought Questions

1. Think back on your own childhood. What was your initial feeling about sex? Was it positive or negative?

2. During your teen years, were you ever head-over-heels in love? Was it love or infatuation?

3. How can you share the beauty of sex with your children in such a way that they will be encouraged to wait until marriage before having sexual relations?

CHAPTER 8

"I Can't Raise This Family Alone!"

(Single Parenting)

> *"I lie awake; I have become like a bird alone on a roof"* (Ps. 102:7, NIV).

Single parents are now in the mainstream of American society, and that fact must be faced by our government, our church, and our family structure.

Despite the negative press and alarming statistics, studies indicate that single parenting can be highly successful and growth-producing in both the parent and children. This is particularly the case when the single parent exerts an effort to sustain a sense of family and the children develop coping skills that will also enhance their adult life. When there is a commitment to living and loving together, there is family. While the single-parent family structure is different from two-parent families, it need not be inferior. Perhaps the three most important elements in any successful family are economic stability, commitment to each family member, and unconditional love. All three can be found in single-parent families.

How much do you really know about raising a family alone? Answer the following true-or-false statements.

1. A single parent should attempt to remarry as soon as possible to provide a better home for the children.

2. Two-parent families function more smoothly and independently than single-parent families.

3. Single parents are most often discriminated against in such areas as housing, finances, education, and employment.

4. Having no father for male children under 6 years of age can impair their identification with men.

5. A good mother always stays at home with her preschool children.

6. It is vital for the child's well-being to feel loved by both parents.

7. Children of divorce most likely are going to have difficulty making their own marriage work.

8. It is appropriate for in-laws to discontinue the relationship with the children and nonblood-related spouse following divorce.

9. Most problems in female-headed households are related to the absence of the father.

10. One out of five children live in a single-parent home.

11. Only single-parent households are fatherless or motherless.

12. A single parent has to make up for the loss of the absent parent. (Answers appear at the end of this chapter.)

Single Parenting Factors

What circumstances create a single-parent family? Two of the most common are being widowed or divorced. A lesser known but sizable portion of single parents occur because of separation. Not all separation is a prelude to divorce. Some spouses may be separated because of work, prison, or other circumstances. It may be temporary or permanent. Another common circumstance is the unwed mother. Statistics indicate an increase in teenage pregnancies and births, which make up a substantial number of never-married single parents.

Ethnic background also plays an important role in determining single-parent families. Recent studies estimate that 19 percent of all White families with children are single-parent households, of which 3 percent have never been married. In the Hispanic community the number of single-parent families increases to 26 percent. But almost 59 percent of Black families are in the single-parent category, and 28 percent have never been married (Ian P. Chand, "A Caring Home in a Caring Church," lecture delivered at Andrews University, June 6, 1989).

Statistics indicate that one of every four families in the United States is a single-parent household and that nine out of every 10 of these is headed by a female parent. Almost half the White children born in the late 1970s will live for some time with a single mother before they reach age 18. However, more than eight out of 10 Black children will share a similar experience.

What about the finances of single-parent families? We used to ask if two could live as cheaply as one. Today we ask if one can live as well as two. With the median income for a female single parent less than half that of a male single parent, it is estimated that six out of every 10 female-headed single-parent families actually live below the poverty level.

Another factor in single-parent families is the distribution of roles. In a two-parent family the roles are often divided according to preference or ability. In a two-parent family the responsibilities may be divided in this manner:

Statistics indicate that one of every four families in the United States is a single-parent household and that nine out of every 10 of these is headed by a female parent. Almost half the White children born in the late 1970s will live for some time with a single mother before they reach age 18. However, more than eight out of 10 Black children will share a similar experience.

Parent A	Parent B
Comforter	Disciplinarian
Emotional stability	Financial stability
Mediator	Decision-maker
Sensitive and understanding	Standards setter and teacher
Maintains family ties	Maintains auto, house, etc.
Partial income provider	Primary income provider
Main child care	Partial child care
Housekeeping service	Arranges outside services
Checkbook balancer	Vacation planner

Obviously many other roles could be added to the parenting list. While each list will probably contain many similarities, it will also be unique in that it is based upon the temperament, culture, and personal expectations of each parent. However, the single parent has a dilemma. All of the above, and more, must be accomplished alone. For example . . .

Parent A	Unmet Needs
Disciplinarian	Comforter [older child?]
Emotional security	Friends [assume greater role]
Housekeeping services	Children [assume greater role]
More self-reliant	Extended family support
Auto driver	Outside maintenance
Primary income provider	Government financial aid
Time constraints	Eat out/prepackaged foods
Standard setter	Children make more decisions

In single-parent families the roles may be more flexible than in a two-parent household. Often pragmatic considerations hold sway over traditional roles or cultural expectations. There may not be a set time for meals. Children may spend more time alone or with friends. Housework may seem less important when it has to be done after work. Child care responsibilities are more likely to be shared. Household chores may be redistributed according to the needs of the family. Financial aid, especially for a female single parent, is almost a necessity.

Single parents also need a support network. Whereas two-parent families usually support each other, the single parent must look further afield. Increased contact with relatives and closer relationships with friends often provide a primary support foundation. Single parents may find a counseling relationship especially helpful after a death or divorce. A professional listener may be more appropriate when single parents feel a compulsion to talk about their feelings. In fact, they may begin to talk more about themselves than about their children.

Joining a support group, such as Parents Without Partners, may provide emotional stability during a time of painful transition. For many, church attendance becomes more meaningful, if they do not experience rejection or apathy. It is tragic that just when single parents need the church family the most, they are sometimes shut out. Some single parents find a support group at work or by taking a class one night a week. It is important that single parents initiate finding their own support network rather than waiting for others to initiate contact.

Single-Parent Feelings

The range of feelings experienced by single parents depends primarily upon their circumstances and temperament blend. Some feel hurt, abandoned, or rejected, whether their partner abandoned them or died. Others suffer from feelings of guilt and inadequacy because they were not able to keep the relationship together or prevent the death of a spouse. Resentment, bitterness, anger, and even rage may be experienced as they review all the wasted years in an unsuccessful relationship. In addition, they may feel bitter because they now have the responsibility to raise the children alone.

In single-parent families the roles may be more flexible than in a two-parent household. Often pragmatic considerations hold sway over traditional roles or cultural expectations.

Some single parents may be able to identify with a lonely Irishman, down on his luck, panhandling the crowd on Fifth Avenue during a Saint Patrick's Day parade. Holding out his hand to a couple strolling by, he said, "May the blessing of the Lord, which brings love and joy and wealth and a fine family, follow you all the days of your life . . ." He paused, expectantly, only to have the couple ignore his outstretched hand as they continued walking down the street. Angrily he shouted after them,". . . and never catch up with you!"

Many single parents have a longing to be close and intimate again. They might even hold on to a fantasy that the relationship will someday be restored. I have counseled with individuals who have been divorced for 10 or 15 years and are still clinging to the fantasy that the former mate will someday return.

Others experience jealousy or envy of their former spouse. They may feel jealous because their former partners have established a new relationship or married and seem to have put their life back together. They may be jealous because the former spouses appear to have a more positive relationship with the children. They may feel jealous because the former spouses have the privilege of being a vacation parent.

The story is told about two divorced parents who were bitter rivals for the attention of their only child. One night an angel appeared in a dream to the more jealous parent. "I will give you anything you request, but know this, your ex-spouse will receive twice as much. You can be rich. You can be healthy. You can be anything you like, but your ex will receive twice as much." Pausing to give the jealous parent time to think, the angel inquired, "What is your desire?"

The jealous parent thought for a few moments and confidently replied, "Strike me blind in one eye!"

Jealousy is a feeling that must be acknowledged and worked through if single parents are to find peace in life. "For jealousy makes a man furious, and he will not spare when he takes revenge" (Prov. 6:34, RSV).

Sometimes a single parent feels like he or she is competing with the other parent for the child's affection and attention. Such parents may go through prolonged periods of self-pity, during which they bemoan all that has befallen them. This is usually followed by feelings of intense relief that they are no longer part of such a painful relationship. To confuse their feelings even more, they may find themselves constantly degrading the person they once loved.

Single parents often experience low self-esteem, emptiness, and depression during their reconstruction period. During this time of uncertainty and negative feelings, they may vacillate between holding on and letting go. During this period these individuals are especially vulnerable to both hurt and affection.

It is important that single parents learn to cope with their flood of negative feelings. How they handle these feelings will largely determine how their children adjust to a new lifestyle. It is not realistic to expect complete control over such negative thoughts and feelings. Only time and prayer can heal all the wounds. Even then there will be lifelong scars as the family readjusts to new responsibilities and lifestyle.

Single parents may feel like the little boy who went to the movie theater with his family. The rest of the family went immediately into the theater to be seated while he lingered in the lobby to purchase popcorn. By the time he arrived inside the theater the lights were already dimming. Walking down the aisle, he scanned the theater for familiar faces. Finally, as the lights dimmed to near-darkness, he stopped and yelled in a plaintive voice, "Does anyone here recognize me?"

Perhaps no word describes the plight of single parents more than "lonely." The quality and quantity of their social life has been drastically altered. Gone are the hugs and kisses. Gone is the emotional security. Gone are the married friends who tried to be helpful (for a while) but really couldn't understand.

Single parents often experience low self-esteem, emptiness, and depression during their reconstruction period. During this time of uncertainty and negative feelings, they may vacillate between holding on and letting go. During this period these individuals are especially vulnerable.

Whether death or divorce has taken away the loved one, single parents need time to work through their personal grief—time to experience and come to terms with the various stages of mourning and time to write another chapter in their book of life. Even though they may have many chapters yet to write, it is best to admit that this one is unpleasant at best. In fact, it is just plain ugly! Grief is like an unwelcome neighbor who has moved in next door, and no matter what you do or where you move, you can't seem to get away.

Grief lives next door to all of us at some time in our life. We must all learn how to let go and move forward without someone or something we wanted very much. Life brings change, and grief always lives next door to change. Grief may pay us an unwelcome visit whenever there is a significant change in our life. Elizabeth Kübler-Ross calls these changes the "little deaths of life." They can include, but are not limited to

moving away from home.
getting married.
getting divorced.

changing jobs.
losing a job.
illness.
children leaving home.
death of a pet.
retirement.
personal growth.
any other significant changes.

How can single parents overcome loneliness during this tumultuous time of change? First of all, they need to accept their feelings and own them. Such feelings belong to these single parents, so they should admit how they feel. It is OK for single parents to admit that they are lonely and that they have negative thoughts that they do not enjoy or even understand at times.

Next, single parents should analyze why they are feeling lonely and determine what they can do about it. Then they can identify and understand their basic needs and desires. It is appropriate for single parents to share as many of their emotions as they feel comfortable sharing with their support network of friends and family. The rest they can share with a professional counselor.

Single parents can learn to anticipate loneliness and take positive steps to thwart its visit. If they know that such feelings arrive during a holiday or special anniversary date, they can fill that time with other friends and activities.

Single parents need not allow themselves to become willing victims of self-pity. They can join a support group to help them through lonely times. They can attend functions sponsored by their support groups. They can attend church and church socials. They can become involved. They can become active in their support groups.

Finally, single parents can make their time alone rewarding. They should do something nice for themselves!

Someone once formulated "Ten Rules for Overcoming Loneliness." Single parents would find it helpful to memorize those rules and recall them whenever they are feeling lonely.

Rule 1: Go out and do something for someone else.

Rule 2: Go out and repeat rule 1 nine times!

Anger is a negative feeling often experienced by single parents. It is a universal reaction to a loss or void in life. When we lose a meaningful relationship, anger becomes an all too familiar companion. Anger is often the companion of

> disappointment.
> rejection.
> hurt.
> being abandoned.
> feeling inadequate.
> not feeling accepted.
> fear of relationships.

Many Christians have never been taught how to deal with their anger. Because they view feelings of anger as unacceptable in a Christian lifestyle, they attempt to deny it. They may often admit to feeling sad and hurt but seldom to feeling angry. For many Christians it is both frightening and disturbing to experience anger. Therefore, they feel it is better to deny the feeling rather than deal with the consequences.

Many Christians have never been taught how to deal with their anger. They may often admit to feeling sad and hurt but seldom to feeling angry. For many Christians it is both frightening and disturbing to experience anger. Therefore, they feel it is better to deny the feeling rather than deal with the consequences.

In case some of the anger does spill out under stress, they either deny that they were angry or feel guilty because they allowed anger to surface. For those who deny their anger it is almost impossible for them to resolve it or their guilt. Such guilt becomes an unbearable burden that threatens their self-esteem and leads into depression.

Other Christians try to suppress their anger. They reason that if it doesn't surface it can cause them no harm. Such suppression often turns their anger inward, and it becomes depression. Inward anger can be turned toward the children in the form of abuse. Inward anger can also cause others to withdraw from their support group (family), which causes them to become lonely.

Often single parents who have been married feel angry toward an ex-spouse, whether divorced or widowed. Angry because they are responsible for raising the children alone. Angry because of the stress created in their new lifestyle. Angry because of the loss of what used to be. Angry at what might have been, should have been, could have been, or would have been.

Mother Teresa was once asked, "Don't you ever become angry at the causes of social injustice that you see in India or in any of the places in which you work?"

Her response was profound in its simplicity: "Why should I expend energy in anger that I can expend in love?"

The negative feelings experienced by single parents can manifest themselves in many physical maladies: headaches or clenched fists, stomach knots or nervous tics, repeated perspiration or hyperventilation, drinking alcohol or taking drugs, overeating or malnutrition, insomnia or inability to get out of bed, gambling, or even having more children to fill the void. All these and more can be reactions to negative feelings.

A woman went to a counselor and expressed her desire to get even with her ex-husband. She told the counselor, "I want to make him as miserable as he has made me!" Hatred dripped from every word.

The counselor thought for a few minutes and suggested, "Go out of your way to do nice things for him. Make it convenient for the children to visit. Use every opportunity to build a lasting friendship. Invite him to share special occasions with you and the children, in your home." Pausing to allow this strange prescription to sink in, the counselor continued, "After six months I want you to come back, and I will tell you how to exact the perfect revenge!"

The woman wasn't sure that she wanted to follow this strange prescription, but she did as the counselor suggested. Six months later she returned. Before the counselor could speak, she blurted out, "I know you are going to tell me how to be as cruel to him as he has been to me, but I just want you to know I'm not interested in finding out. The children and I have never gotten along better. I just got a promotion at work, and I haven't felt better in years. Even my ex doesn't seem like such a jerk anymore. I just want to leave well enough alone."

"If your enemy is hungry, give him food to eat; if he is thirsty, give him water to drink. . . . And the Lord will reward you" (Prov. 25:21, 22, NIV).

Single Parenting and Relationships

Fear commonly prevents people from building new relationships. Besides their own insecurity, single parents have the children to consider. How will the children view another adult in their world? Will the other parent use this new relationship to turn the children against him or her?

Single parents can begin seeking a new relationship by admitting their needs—the need for emotional attachment or security, the need for sexual intimacy, the need to feel fulfilled and valuable. With admission comes the possibility of fulfillment.

Once single parents admit their needs, they can try out their relationship abilities with their closest friends by spending more time with them (without smothering) and by deepening the friendship. Family and work associates can provide other opportunities for building relationships. The church family is a likely source, but single parents should not be dismayed if they must make the first, second, or even third advance. Some people do not know how to talk to others who are suffering through such experiences—especially if they have never experienced it themselves. Support groups will also provide an opportunity for building new and positive relationships.

It is important that single parents learn to enjoy themselves. They can evaluate their positive temperament traits and spiritual gifts and dedicate them to God so they can bring healing to others. We all experience personal fulfillment even as we minister to others.

It is important that single parents learn to enjoy themselves. They can evaluate their positive temperament traits and spiritual gifts and dedicate them to God so they can bring healing to others. We all experience personal fulfillment even as we minister to others.

Once single parents have regained their confidence and the hurting has subsided, they may wish to consider dating. There are many positive reasons dating is recommended for single parents. First of all, it offers a diversion and an opportunity to establish new relationships. The affirmation of others always enhances our own confidence. As the self-worth of single parents increases, their loneliness will decrease. By experimenting with different relationships, they may even find a lifelong mate. At the very least, dating will establish an extended social network that offers a variety of new interests, and it may result in a loving lifelong companion.

Some single parents refuse to date because their children disapprove. Such objections should be viewed as an opportunity to help them work through their own inner anger and pain.

Single parents should talk to the children about their negative behavior—at a time when it is not occurring, of course. They can look directly into their eyes and keep smiling compassionately while they address the issue.

It is important for children to learn that whatever happened between their parents, it has not ended relationships with members of the opposite sex. Single parents should convey the message that love and happiness are still possible.

Single parents can help their children put their feelings into words—without prying or criticizing. "You seem pretty grouchy when I'm with X. Maybe I'm wrong, but I wonder if you're acting that way because you feel left out."

Single parents will try to understand their children's feelings. They can empathize and verbalize. "Do you feel left out? I can understand that. I bet it's hard for you to see me laughing and enjoying myself with any man [or woman]."

They should ask about the children's behavior and show approval when they receive an honest answer. "How do you act when you feel left out?"

They can explore the effect of the children's behavior on others, helping them understand how it affects others. "When you act this way, I feel . . ."

Single parents can reach agreements for new behaviors at specific times and places! "OK, when X comes over today, how are you going to behave? Fine. Let's shake on it."

With lots of smiles and hugs, single parents can reward their children for improved behavior.

It is important for children to learn that whatever happened between their parents, it has not ended relationships with members of the opposite sex. Single parents should convey the message that love and happiness are still possible. Mistakes are correctable. Humans are fallible and forgivable. We all need other people in our life.

Suggestions for Single Parents

Single parents need to allow time for adjustment. It will usually take at least a year before they are ready to consider another relationship seriously. I would strongly recommend that single parents not even consider marriage for at least a year. Any dating during that time should be casual. Most freshman single parents do not fully realize their vulnerability at this point.

Less than six months after his divorce a good friend of mine decided to marry the first woman he dated. No matter how hard we tried to talk him out of it, he insisted he knew what he was doing. After he dated the young woman for fewer than six weeks they got married. The marriage lasted less than a year. The relapse was much worse than his original condition.

None of us need ever walk alone. God is always there to soothe the hurts and heal the wounds. All of us are part of His family. Let us rejoice and enjoy it!

During this vulnerable time it is important for single parents to maintain contact with established friends. Some single parents are tempted to cut themselves off from old friends because they feel like a failure. This is a tragic mistake. Rather than cut themselves off from past friendships, they should work to strengthen them. This is a lot safer than pursuing new relationships during the first year of single parenting.

Single parents, of course, will reconfirm God in their lives by recommitting themselves to God and spending time with Him each day. None of us need ever walk alone. God is always there to soothe the hurts and heal the wounds. All of us are part of His family. Let us rejoice and enjoy it!

"See how very much our heavenly Father loves us, for he allows us to be called his children—think of it—and we really *are!*" "Dear friends, let us practice loving each other, for love comes from God and those who are loving and kind show that they are the children of God, and that they are getting to know him better" (1 John 3:1; 4:7, TLB).

Single parents—like all of us—will want to make family worship a coveted time each day, rather than a boring exercise that both they and the children dread. They can visit Christian bookstores for ideas and purchase or borrow children's storybooks, cassettes, and videotapes to make worships special. They will seek God's guidance in their daily activities. Then each time they catch a glimpse of the Master's intervention during the day, they may wish to offer a brief praise prayer. Some single parents may choose to write down a few of these instances of divine guidance so they can share them at family worship. Even the children may choose to keep a list and recall at least one glimpse of God's care each day.

Single parents may wish to encourage fellow church members to become more involved with their family, letting others take the children to the park while they do something special. They can allow their children to spend a weekend with a special family in the church. In addition, the children will gain role models as they are exposed to the sex opposite the single parent.

Single parents need not feel awkward about seeking support from friends, family, fellow church members, support groups, and professionals. It is not a sign of weakness to seek help when we are hurting. The greatest joys in life often occur while we are giving to others in need. This applies also to spiritual gifts. We need not deny someone with the gift of listening the joy of ministering to us in Christ. However, we may need to take the first step and make that person aware of our needs.

Single parents may wish to encourage fellow church members to become more involved with their family, letting others take the children to the park while they do something special. They can allow their children to spend a weekend with a special family in the church. Some single parents form a baby-sitting club in their church. Such clubs can provide positive baby-sitting alternates that cost nothing. In addition, the children will gain role models as they are exposed to the sex opposite the single parent.

Not just single parents alone but all of us need to learn to trust God to bring special people into our children's lives as proper role models. God brought Paul into the life of a young man being raised by his mother and grandmother. Evidently Timothy's father was not home very much, nor was he a Christian. Paul became Timothy's mentor, father, and friend. So close was their relationship that Paul referred to Timothy as his "dear son."

As single parents examine their motives and actions, they can ask themselves, "Do my actions stem from self-pity, jealousy, revenge, or guilt?" If so, these attitudes must be changed before they can build successful relationships. God forgives our negative thoughts and can replace them with positive affirmations. Single parents can claim 1 John 1:9 as their promise from God, rewriting the text so it applies directly to them: "If I confess my sins, God is faithful and just, and will forgive my sins and cleanse me from all unrighteousness."

It is important for single parents not to allow themselves to get caught in the guilt trap. In my many years of counseling I have never met a completely innocent party in a broken relationship. In my experience, both parties appear to have contributed to the failure or success of the relationship. It is usually an exercise in futility to try to determine the degree of guilt or innocence of either party.

Single parents should stop carrying around guilt as their constant companion. Jesus bore our guilt on His cross, and we do not need to put it on our back again.

So single parents should stop carrying around guilt as their constant companion. Jesus bore our guilt on His cross, and we do not need to put it on our back again. We can leave it on the cross. God has forgiven. We don't have to allow guilt and self-pity to destroy our new beginnings.

Single parents can learn to remember the best parts of their marriage while not living in the past. They can share pleasant memories with the children and use them to build new relationships. They can try to avoid situations that trigger negative memories, and when negative recollections appear on the memory screen, they can erase them. "As [a man] thinketh in his heart, so is he" (Prov. 23:7).

When single parents share some of their feelings with their children and encourage the children to share with them, they should be cautious that they do not impose their feelings upon the children. The children should be allowed to have their own feelings. Wise parents—single or otherwise—do not demand that their children share confidences.

The feelings and perceptions of children for their parents are never the same as the feelings of parents for each other. Both adults and children need time for the wounds to heal before talking about them. There is no need to rush or pry. But parents can make themselves available and share their own feelings in appropriate ways.

Single parents should be realistic about themselves, the other parent, the children, and their own responsibilities. They shouldn't overprotect the children as though nothing has changed; instead, they should let them know that there may be difficult times ahead. And when it comes time to send the children to college, the family will probably need to work out some kind of creative financing. Single parents can share responsibilities with their children and work together to achieve common goals. If the children learn cooperation, they will have mastered one of the great lessons of life.

No one is completely good or completely bad. We all stand in need of God's salvation. Forgiveness is a gift from God that we have the privilege of sharing with others.

Single parents should allow the children to love and respect the other parent. They should not belittle or put down the other parent. They should not condemn the children if their behavior reminds them of the other parent. It is important to learn to criticize an action that is not condoned but not the person.

One woman's husband left her for another woman and continued to have frequent affairs. She was separated from her husband but not yet divorced. Speaking to her three school-age children, she said, "We need to pray for Daddy right now because he is really mixed up and doing some wrong things."

Parents can use such opportunities to teach their children about the realities of sin. God created us in His image, but we have fallen a long way since the first family in Eden. We can let children know that all have sinned—not just the erring spouse. No one is completely good or completely bad. We all stand in need of God's salvation. Forgiveness is a gift from God that we have the privilege of sharing with others.

Single parents should reassure the children that the other parent still loves them. A parent's complaints may be interpreted as rejection when the children share them with the other parent. However, single parents should be honest with the children when the other parent fails to follow through with promises or visits. On such occasions it is helpful to keep the information brief and simple. Children need permission to love both parents freely and should not feel guilty for doing so.

Since stability is important during times of stress, single parents will want, as far as possible, to keep the same home, friends, school, and routine. Church attendance will provide not only stability but support.

Single parents need to think of themselves as individuals rather than as part of someone else. The value they learn to place on themselves will be reflected in the lives of their children and the relationship of friends.

There is nothing wrong in using one's single status as an opportunity for personal growth and development. All of us—especially single parents—should make each day count by trying something new. Single parents should be alert to make new friends and acquaintances, actively reaching out to other people. They can get involved in activities outside the home or workplace. They can endeavor to contemplate and understand God's personal love for them and their family.

If Jesus had been born 2,000 years later and in our Western culture, He might have worded His model prayer a little differently. If, on that day, He had been ministering to single parents, He might have suggested a prayer like this:

> Our Father
> who lives in heaven,
> where it's much quieter than it is in our hectic home,
> Your kingdom come,
> Your will be done.
> But meanwhile single parents surely need Your special help.
> Give us this day our daily ration of wisdom,
> and forgive us our mistakes
> as we forgive the mistakes of our children.
> And lead us not into vexation,
> but deliver us from despair.

For to You belong the babies,
and the children, and the teenagers, and all parents
now and forever.
Amen.

Answers to the Single-Parent Quiz:

1. *False.* It is important to have time and space to adjust to the loss of a partner and past way of life. For at least a year marriage and even serious dating is not advisable.

2. *False.* Both family systems face similar issues relating to finances, feelings of inadequacy, dependence, communication, and other common causes of contention.

3. *True.*

4. *False.* It is important for their development that both boys and girls have male role-models. However, these men can be relatives, friends, teachers, etc.

5. *False.* Consistent nurturing and stable child care is vitally important, but this can be provided in a good day-care center, at home, or in someone else's home by a caring, reliable adult. Good mothers may stay at home or go to work, depending on their needs and the needs of the family. Would this even be asked if the father has custody? What about two-income families?

6. *False.* This is important and helpful, but not vital. As long as children feel that they are loved and lovable, the love can come from many different people.

7. *False.* Children need to have positive models of men and women who communicate well with each other, but children can learn about communication from parents in their other relationships, as well as from other people.

8. *False.* It is important that all family members, no matter which side they belong to, maintain contact with children, because children feel more secure and whole if they have ongoing relationships with these people.

9. *False.* Problems are more related to poverty, and bad neighborhoods with increased crime rate, exposure to drugs, bad schools, and low wage-earning capacity (female-headed households have less than 50 percent of the income of male-headed—even though both are single parents).

10. *True.*

11. *False.* Fathers and mothers in two-parent families are often physically or emotionally unavailable, away on business, involved in many outside activities, hiding behind newspapers or the television.

12. *False.* In today's world, distinctions between fathers' roles and mothers' roles are not as clear-cut as they used to be. Also, children turn to role modeling and support outside the home through extended family, peers, teachers, youth leaders, and other admired adults.

Thought Questions

1. Reflect on how the priorities of a single-parent family might differ from those of a two-parent family.

2. Can you recall a time in your past when grief and loneliness caused you intense pain? How can that experience help you identify with single parents?

3. Can you think of at least five ways to make God first in your life?

CHAPTER 9

"Things Just Aren't Like They Used to Be When I Was a Kid!"

(The Adventist Family Enters the Twenty-first Century)

> *"God would have our families symbols of the family in heaven. Let parents and children bear this in mind every day, relating themselves to one another as members of the family of God"* (Ellen G. White, The Adventist Home, *p. 17*).

Have you ever wondered what phrases your neighbors might use to describe your family to the rest of the neighborhood? If you are an Adventist family, they might say something like:

"Oh, they're the family that doesn't eat any meat."

Actually, fewer than half the Seventh-day Adventist families in the U.S. would fit that description. The number of Adventists who follow a strict or modified vegetarian diet comprise a relatively small portion of the total number of Adventists or vegetarians in the United States.

"They must be the family that's always talking about sending their kids to college."

That statement is quite accurate. Two thirds of all Adventist males are professional, managerial, or white collar workers. One third of all Adventist females have a college degree, and an incredible 50 percent of all baby-boomer males have earned their sheepskin (*Adventist Family Opinion: Demographic Profile*).

"They're the family with the mortgage payments."

Yes, that's true. Seventh-day Adventists are more likely to live in single-family dwellings and own their home than the general population in the U.S.

"They're the traditional family—where Dad is off at work and Mom is staying home to raise the kids."

Not anymore. Three out of every four Adventist women of working age are employed outside the home.

"They're the family that insists on paying cash for everything."

Not at all. Adventists are twice as likely to have credit cards as the general population.

"They're the family that doesn't own a TV."

Wrong again. Adventist ownership of TVs and VCRs is about the same as the general population.

"They're the family that spends a lot of quality time together."

That's a nice thought, but unfortunately, it does not appear to be true. The Adventist divorce rate and the number of single-parent families is about the same percentage as that of the general population. If we are spending quality time together, it doesn't show.

"They're the family with all the kids."

Adventists are twice as likely to have credit cards as the general population.

Even though 72 percent of all Seventh-day Adventists are married, only 35 percent actually have children, and two out of five of those couples with children do not have children in their home (i.e., empty-nest families, etc.). In addition, the Adventist birth rate is lower than that of the general population.

"They're the family that attends that 'old people's' church."

In a recent survey of Maryland, the District of Columbia, and Virginia, 54 percent of the members were between the ages of 20 and 49. Throughout the U.S. 40 percent of Adventist members are in that same age category. About 15 percent of Adventist membership is over the age of 65 because of a healthier lifestyle than that practiced by the general populace (*Adventist Family Needs Survey*).

"They're the couple always complaining about their marriage."

Definitely not. The same East Coast survey indicated that 86 percent of Seventh-day Adventists rate their marriage good to excellent (41 percent excellent; 27 percent very good; and 18 percent good). However, even though we don't complain, our divorce rate is comparable to the national average.

"They're the family that moved out of the city into the country."

Not really. Adventists have only moved to the suburbs. Fully half of all Adventist families live in urban-suburban areas. Only one in five families lives in a rural setting.

What does all this mean? It means that the stereotype of Seventh-day Adventists is no longer true. It means that we are entering the twenty-first century whether we like it or not. It means that our children see a different family structure than we might have grown up with. It means that Adventist families are different not only from other Christian families but also from previous generations.

It is time for us to reaffirm the three major building blocks that make the Adventist family unique: (1) Sabbath, (2) sanctuary, and (3) Spirit of Prophecy.

It is time for us to reaffirm the three major building blocks that make the Adventist family unique: (1) Sabbath, (2) sanctuary, and (3) Spirit of Prophecy.

Sabbath

The seventh-day Sabbath provides a unique building block for the Adventist family. Even though there is a substantial Jewish population that worships on Sabbath (as well as smaller Christian groups), Adventists are the only major Christian group that observes Saturday as the Sabbath. The Sabbath definitely causes Adventist families to stand out from the rest of their community. It also presents some unique challenges for raising a family in an environment in which Sunday is viewed as the accepted day of rest.

I became an Adventist as an adult and remember vividly my very first Sabbath as a member of the church. It was very difficult for me. I must confess that I was more interested in not displeasing God than I was in pleasing Him. I did not want to break the Sabbath, so I spent the entire afternoon sitting in a rocking chair as I read my Bible. I didn't know what else to do.

Our 5-year-old son was forced to take a nap and be quiet, even though he wasn't sleepy and wanted to talk. As I look back on that experience, it certainly was unique! Yet it was not the kind of uniqueness I would want our son to model. We were not functional as a Sabbath family.

Later I read: "The Sabbath should be made so interesting to our families that its weekly return will be hailed with joy" (*Testimonies*, vol. 2, p. 585).

"All who love God should do what they can to make the Sabbath a delight, holy and honorable. . . . They can do much to exalt the Sabbath in their families and make it the most interesting day of the week" (*ibid.*, p. 584).

Some families find the Sabbath hours to be a mixed blessing. While they are worshiping in church, most of America is shopping, cleaning, repairing, and mowing. This causes some families to feel more out of step than unique. Therefore, for some Adventist families the Sabbath may actually seem to be more of an inconvenience than a blessing.

"The Sabbath was made for man, to be a blessing to him by calling his mind from secular labor to contemplate the goodness and glory of God. It is necessary that the people of God assemble to talk of Him, to interchange thoughts and ideas in regard to the truths contained in His Word, and to devote a portion of time to appropriate prayer. But these seasons, even upon the Sabbath, should not be made tedious by their length and lack of interest" (*ibid.*, p. 583).

"The Sabbath should be made so interesting to our families that its weekly return will be hailed with joy."

While we lived in Bloemfontein, South Africa, I became acutely aware of how inconvenient the Sabbath could be. All the stores closed at 5:00 p.m. each day and remained closed all day on Sunday. The biggest shopping day was obviously Saturday. Our working schedule made it difficult for us to do our necessary shopping. In that sense, the Sabbath was inconvenient. But we found a way to get everything done, and were actually grateful that we weren't involved in the mad shopping rush on Saturday.

Even recreation can sometimes be a problem for Sabbathkeeping families. Karen and I really enjoy playing tennis. When we moved to South Africa, we were delighted to discover a tennis club just a few blocks from our home. We joined the club soon after our arrival. The first Sunday after joining, Karen and I arrived early at the courts and were amazed that no one was using them. Gleefully we began playing, enjoying the freedom of having the entire complex to ourselves.

About 9:00 a.m. the bells began ringing at the church across the street.

Soon people were walking by the tennis courts on their way to church. We were perplexed because almost every person gave us a hostile stare. Later we learned that it was illegal to play tennis in Bloemfontein on Sunday.

Whether or not the Sabbath is inconvenient is actually a matter of attitude. While it may appear to restrict in some areas, it actually frees us to be a family. Sabbath provides quality family time when we can really get to know each other and our God. Sabbath provides an opportunity for us to witness together as a family by visiting our neighbors and friends. Sabbath influences us to lay down our burdens and relax with God and each other. Sabbath is God-given protection from the stress of everyday living and the uncertainty of entering the twenty-first century.

It is important for every family to determine what Sabbathkeeping means to them. Study the Scripture and Spirit of Prophecy. Make an outline of Sabbath principles and privileges. Determine to make the Sabbath a delight rather than an inconvenience. Rather than voicing what you cannot do on the Sabbath, use your family council to plan special activities for that day only. God reminds us to make the Sabbath a *delight*, not a drag. When teens refuse to attend church, it is often because the Sabbath has been a drag for years and they found little delight in spending time with their family or God. Do not major in minutia when planning Sabbath activities. *How* you spend the day is more important than *what* you are doing.

> **Determine to make the Sabbath a delight rather than an inconvenience. God reminds us to make the Sabbath a delight, not a drag. Do not major in minutia when planning Sabbath activities. *How* you spend the day is more important than *what* you are doing.**

The Sabbath offers a special time for family bonding at least one day a week. Our family was involved in college at a time when most families are pursuing their careers. I was 30 something when I entered college for the first time. It was difficult to fulfill all our financial, study, and family obligations. We all looked forward to Friday nights, when there would be no studies, no television, no bills, and no distractions. Our apartment had a little fireplace, and it became a family tradition to lie in front of the fire and talk after supper. It was family time. It was bonding time. Bonding requires commitment, sharing, and time. Most of all, time.

A busy yuppie father discovered he had cancer. Not knowing how to break the news to his family, he reserved an entire evening in his appointment book for the occasion. When the evening was over, he realized how much he had enjoyed their time together, even though it involved sharing bad news. He checked his calendar to see when he could schedule another family evening. To his dismay, he found that he could not fit it into his schedule for at least a year. He then sadly reflected, "No one on his deathbed ever said, 'I wish I had spent more time on my job.'"

For the Adventist family, God has written a weekly appointment into the date book. It is automatic. It is family time. It is God's love gift to us.

"The Sabbath and the family were alike instituted in Eden, and in God's purpose they are indissolubly linked together. On this day more than on any other, it is possible for us to live the life of Eden" (Ellen G. White, *Education*, p. 250).

"The Sabbath and the family were alike instituted in Eden, and in God's purpose they are indissolubly linked together. On this day more than on any other, it is possible for us to live the life of Eden."

Sanctuary

Another building block of the Adventist family is our understanding of God's sanctuary both in heaven and on earth. There is a common bond between the sanctuary and the family.

"The house is the sanctuary for the family, and the closet or the grove the most retired place for individual worship; but the church is the sanctuary for the congregation" (*Testimonies*, vol. 5, p. 491).

God gave His people the sanctuary to illustrate in dramatic fashion the plan of salvation. This plan was illustrated with festivals and events that brought God's family together. Likewise, God uses the family sanctuary to illustrate His plan of salvation. It is in the family sanctuary that we learn the lessons of life. It is in this environment that God becomes a loving and forgiving father. It is in the family sanctuary that our character is formed and our disposition determined.

"If you would be a saint in heaven, you must first be a saint on earth. . . . You will come up from the grave with the same disposition you manifested in your home and in society" (*The Adventist Home*, p. 16).

A young family invited the new preacher and his wife home for dinner after church. Mother was very concerned that all the children be on their very best behavior. She wanted to make a good impression. The table was beautifully set with her best china. The linen napkins were folded in a beautiful fan shape on each plate. The food was deliciously prepared and attractively served. She had even made a lovely centerpiece, complete with lighted candles.

All bowed their heads as Father asked God's blessing upon the food and their fellowship together. When it was over, the 9-year-old girl reached for her glass of iced herbal tea and knocked it over. Little brother jumped to get out of the way of the cascading liquid and knocked his glass over too. There was an awkward moment of silence as everyone looked at Mother. Disappointment was written all over her face.

"If you would be a saint in heaven, you must first be a saint on earth. . . . You will come up from the grave with the same disposition you manifested in your home and in society."

Before anyone could say anything, Father flipped over his glass of tea and began to laugh. The preacher caught on and flipped over his glass of tea as he joined in the laughter. The preacher's wife likewise knocked over her glass of tea and giggled. Everyone looked back at Mother, who finally, with an expression of resignation, picked up her glass and just dumped it out in the middle of the table.

Everyone around the table just roared with laughter. Father looked down at his 9-year-old daughter seated beside him and gave her a wink. As she laughed embarrassingly, she looked up at her father and winked back. As she did, it flicked a tear out onto her cheek, and it rolled slowly down her face. She continued to look up, almost worshipfully, at her father, who loved her enough to save her from one of life's most embarrassing moments.

In a setting of love the family sanctuary truly becomes an object lesson of salvation. The family sanctuary is where both children and parents learn the lessons of life. Family is where character is formed and lasting impressions are made. "In a sense the father is the priest of the household, laying upon the family altar the morning and evening sacrifice" (*The Ministry of Healing*, p. 392).

Because of parental concern and the desire to teach their young son responsibility, a young boy was required to phone home when he arrived at his friend's house a few blocks away. As the boy's confidence increased, his memory decreased, and he frequently forgot to call home. This meant that Father or Mother had to call to see if he had arrived safely.

Concerned that their son was not learning to be responsible, they told him that the next time he forgot to call home he would have to return home immediately when they phoned.

A few days later the boy went to visit his friend and forgot to call home. Father did not wish to punish him, just make him responsible. Trying to think what to do, he prayed for wisdom. As he dialed, the Lord seemed to keep saying to him, "Treat him like I treat you." Just as the telephone rang for the first time, the father hung up.

A few seconds later his phone rang. "I'm here, Dad!" the son said breathlessly.

"What took you so long to call?" inquired the father.

"We started playing and I forgot. But, Dad, I heard the phone ring once and I remembered."

I wonder how many times God lets the phone ring just once for mothers and fathers, hoping that we too will call home.

A sad statistic is that 28 percent of runaway children in America have actually been forced out of their homes by their parents. Of Americans listed as missing persons, nearly 80 percent of them are under the age of 18. Divorce has been a major factor in the rising number of abandoned teens. The divorce rate is almost 250 percent higher today than it was in 1960. This has increased the number of those cohabiting together outside of marriage as well as the number of stepfamily units.

"In 1987 about 9 million children under 18 years of age were in stepfamilies, with 6 million being stepchildren born before the remarriage and 3 million born after the remarriage" (Paul C. Glick, *The Family Life Cycle and Social Change*, p. 126).

Sometimes teens have difficulty adjusting to their new stepparent. Such tension can lead to the teen leaving home. Even though staying together for the sake of the children may not always be in the children's best interests, parents are still responsible for their welfare after a divorce. Parents often separate and remarry without considering their children's needs. As one writer lamented: "We have been so anxious to give our children what we didn't have that we have neglected to give them what we did have" (*Encounter*, May 1982).

God designed that the family sanctuary was to be a place of refuge—a safe harbor in which to weather the storms of life. What God has joined together, too many parents today are tearing asunder.

"We have been so anxious to give our children what we didn't have that we have neglected to give them what we did have."

The author of *Twenty-One Stayed* tells the story of 21 American soldiers who were captured by the enemy during the Korean War and who later defected to their captors. They chose not to return to the U.S. after the truce was signed. Research by the author revealed that 19 of the 21 soldiers had felt unloved or unwanted by their fathers. A child is not likely to find a father in God unless he first finds something of God in his father.

Spirit of Prophecy

This final building block in the family foundation is unique to Seventh-day Adventists. While other denominations have a prophet, Adventists believe that God inspired Ellen G. White to lead His people back to the Bible. "Little heed is given to the Bible, and the Lord has given a lesser light to lead men and women to the greater light" (Ellen G. White, in *Review and Herald*, Jan. 20, 1903, p. 15).

Mrs. White continually referred to the Bible as the guidebook for every family. "I recommend to you, dear reader, the Word of God as the rule of your faith and practice. By that Word we are to be judged. God has, in that Word, promised to give visions in the '*last days*'; not for a new rule of faith, but for the comfort of His people, and to correct those who err from Bible truth" (*Early Writings*, p. 78).

Unfortunately, the purpose of God's messenger has often been misunderstood, even by those who claimed to be her most ardent supporters (White, in *Review and Herald*, Aug. 30, 1906, p. 8).

Some parents have used the writings of Ellen White more in a spirit of discipline rather than prophecy. This is, indeed, unfortunate since during her lifetime Mrs. White offered a rich variety of counsel on many topics, including the Adventist family.

"Every family is a church, over which the parents preside. The first consideration of the parents should be to work for the salvation of their children. When the father and mother as priest and teacher of the family take their position fully on the side of Christ, a good influence will be exerted in the home. And this sanctified influence will be felt in the church and will be recognized by every believer" (Ellen G. White, *Child Guidance*, p. 549).

"Remember that just as you are in your family, so will you be in the church. Just as you treat your children, so will you treat Christ. If you cherish an un-Christlike spirit, you are dishonoring God" (*The Seventh-day Adventist Bible Commentary*, Ellen G. White Comments, vol. 5, p. 1131).

> **"Remember that just as you are in your family, so will you be in the church. Just as you treat your children, so will you treat Christ. If you cherish an un-Christlike spirit, you are dishonoring God."**

The uniqueness of the Adventist family is more than a high percentage of college degrees, white-collar workers, credit cards, or mortgage payments. Perhaps the real uniqueness of Adventist families today will be their ability to model the Sabbath, sanctuary, and Spirit of Prophecy as we enter the twenty-first century.

However, in order to be such a model, many modern Adventist families need to reevaluate their priorities. Families need to spend enough time together to prevent broken homes and estranged children. Divorce rates among Adventist couples should be much lower than that of the general population. The uniqueness of the Adventist message is meaningless unless it fosters commitment and lasting relationships.

Families are like a house. If they are to last, they must be built on a solid foundation. God has graciously provided for Seventh-day Adventist families reinforcement not readily available to many others. He has set aside special family time each week for bonding with each other and with Him. God urges us to view our family as a sanctuary in which the plan of salvation is acted out daily in our lives. And to make certain our families have every advantage, God inspired a woman in our own century to write a potpourri on family relations and commitment.

Rather than lamenting the demise of the traditional family (which may have been based more on fantasy than fact), the modern Adventist family should be challenged to build upon the foundation given by God for His remnant people: the Sabbath, the sanctuary, and the Spirit of Prophecy. When Adventist families become living object lessons, then perhaps they will one day become the norm for our society, as God intended.

"The greatest evidence of the power of Christianity that can be presented to the world is a well-ordered, well-disciplined family. This will recommend the truth as nothing else can, for it is a living witness of its practical power upon the heart" (*Testimonies*, vol. 4, p. 304).

> **"The greatest evidence of the power of Christianity that can be presented to the world is a well-ordered, well-disciplined family. This will recommend the truth as nothing else can, for it is a living witness of its practical power upon the heart"** (*Testimonies*, vol. 4, p. 304).

Thought Questions

1. How does your family compare to the statements made about the "average" Adventist family?

2. Would you describe your home as a sanctuary? Explain.

3. Recall your childhood. If you were raised in an Adventist home, did you look forward to the Sabbath each week, or regret its coming? What about your children?

More Books for Parents

Family Fun

Darlene McRoberts provides hundreds of ideas for creating happy memories with young children. Includes simple worship activities, easy-to-do craft projects, holiday celebrations for Christians, and fun-filled nature adventures. Paper, 80 pages. US$6.95, Cdn$8.70.

Kids: How You Shape Their Lives

Drawing from 27 years' experience as a teacher, Ruth Buntain gives practical counsel on child rearing, with emphasis on imparting emotional and spiritual strength to the child. Paper, 78 pages. US$6.50, Cdn$8.10.

Passing On the Torch

Roger Dudley reveals how to pass on spiritual values to children and teens successfully. Hardcover, 192 pages. US$13.95, Cdn$17.45. Paper, 192 pages. US$10.95, Cdn$13.70.

Teaching Old-fashioned Values to New-fashioned Kids

Basing her advice on the Bible and Spirit of Prophecy, Josephine Cunnington Edwards shows how to teach children Christian values, manners, and love for God. Paper, 120 pages. US$6.95, Cdn$8.70.

To order, call **1-800-765-6955** or write to ABC Mailing Service, P.O. Box 1119, Hagerstown, MD 21741. Send check or money order. Enclose applicable sales tax and 15 percent (minimum US$2.50) for postage and handling. Prices and availability subject to change without notice. Add GST in Canada.

Practical Help for Young Mothers

Help! I'm a Mother!

Drawing from years of experience as a mother and OB nurse, Nancy Beck Irland offers sensitive advice on how to cope with motherhood. Emotional adjustment for mom, a baby's different cries, what to do when the baby is sick, adjusting to the second and third baby—and much more—are covered in this practical book. Paper, 96 pages. US$6.95, Cdn$8.70.

The Making of a Mother

Karen Spruill writes a surprisingly frank and personal book about motherhood. She shares her secret battles with frustration and feelings of inadequacy. Then she tells what it took to set her free. She also gives tried-and-true advice on breast feeding, toilet training, self-forgiveness, and money matters. "The chapter on discipline alone is worth the price of the book," says fellow author and mother June Strong. Paper, 128 pages. US$7.95, Cdn$9.95.

Time Out for Moms

Cheryl Woolsey Holloway's delightful devotional book for young mothers bubbles over with warmth and sparkling humor. She shares moments drawn from her family life that have resulted in self-discovery, growth, adjustment, intense love, and turmoil. Mothers will find encouragement and strength and enjoy the rare luxury of being nurtured. Paper, 94 pages. US$6.95, Cdn$8.70.

To order, call **1-800-765-6955** or write to ABC Mailing Service, P.O. Box 1119, Hagerstown, MD 21741. Send check or money order. Enclose applicable sales tax and 15 percent (minimum US$2.50) for postage and handling. Prices and availability subject to change without notice. Add GST in Canada.